LANGUAGE
AND RESPONSIBILITY

Also by Noam Chomsky

American Power and the New Mandarins

At War with Asia: *Essays on Indochina*

Problems of Knowledge and Freedom:
The Russell Lectures

For Reasons of State

Peace in the Middle East?
Reflections on Justice and Nationhood

Reflections on Language

LANGUAGE
AND
RESPONSIBILITY

NOAM CHOMSKY

Based on conversations
with Mitsou Ronat

Translated from the French by John Viertel

PANTHEON BOOKS
New York

Library of Congress Cataloging in Publication Data

Chomsky, Noam.

Language and Responsibility.

Translation of *Dialogues avec Mitsou Ronat*.
Includes index.
1. Languages—Political aspects.
2. Generative grammar. I. Ronat, Mitsou.
II. Title.
P120.P64C513   1979   415   78-53921
ISBN 0-394-42650-9
ISBN 0-394-73619-2 pbk.

Manufactured in the United States of America

FIRST AMERICAN EDITION

Contents

TRANSLATOR'S NOTE   vii

INTRODUCTORY COMMENT   ix

PART I   Linguistics and Politics   1

Chapter 1. *Politics*   3
Chapter 2. *Linguistics and the Human Sciences*   43
Chapter 3. *A Philosophy of Language?*   63
Chapter 4. *Empiricism and Rationalism*   81

PART II   Generative Grammar   101

Chapter 5. *The Birth of Generative Grammar*   103
Chapter 6. *Semantics*   136
Chapter 7. *The Extended Standard Theory*   163
Chapter 8. *Deep Structure*   169
Chapter 9. *Universal Grammar and Unresolved Questions*   180

NOTES   195

INDEX   199

Translator's Note

That my name appears as translator of a book by Noam Chomsky into English obviously requires an explanation.

The origin of this book lies in conversations between Chomsky and the French linguist Mitsou Ronat, carried on in English on his part, in French on hers. The conversations were recorded on tape, and Mitsou Ronat published them in France after translating Chomsky into French (Noam Chomsky, *Dialogues avec Mitsou Ronat,* Paris, 1977).

When Pantheon then planned publication of this book in the United States, Chomsky asked me to prepare an "English version." As the passages contributed by Mitsou Ronat were originally in French, these constituted a straightforward task of translation. However, the French translation of Chomsky presented quite a different problem. The original tapes were no longer available. I felt a bit as if, say, one of Shakespeare's plays had been lost and only the (very excellent) German translation of Schlegel and Tieck had survived, and the problem now was to prepare an English text on that basis. The task was rendered somewhat less formidable by Chomsky's willingness to go over my "translation" very carefully and to correct it. As it turned out, in doing so he also made substantial revisions in the text.

Thus, as far as this portion of the book—the major portion by far—is concerned, what the title page should actually say is: "reconstructed with the aid of . . ." rather than "translated by . . . ." Of course, it is possible that in spite of the great pains he took, some errors still escaped Chomsky's notice; for these, I'm afraid, I must accept entire responsibility.

In spite of these difficulties, I enjoyed the work more than any translation I have ever undertaken: because of the content—the

first chapter on political questions and on the student movement of the 1960s said so many things which needed to be said
—and also because I believe the book presents the clearest
exposition yet of Chomsky's basic conceptions in linguistics and
related issues in philosophy, psychology, and social studies. It
offers an excellent introduction to those not familiar with
Chomsky's linguistic work and the generative grammar approach. At the same time, it provides a comprehensive overview
of the various aspects of generative grammar and the present
state of research that should be of interest to linguists, philosophers, and others who have more familiarity with these questions.

Introductory Comment

The material that follows is based on conversations held in January 1976, conducted partly in French, partly in English. The transcript was published in French translation in 1977. Retranslation into English posed a number of problems, among them, the difficulty of reconstructing the original. In the course of reviewing the translation I introduced a number of stylistic and sometimes substantive changes, adding passages to clarify or extend what was said. Thus the present book, while preserving the basic structure of the original, is not simply a translation of the French translation of my remarks, but is rather an elaboration and in some cases modification of the French version.

Noam Chomsky
Cambridge, Mass.
April 1978

PART I

Linguistics and Politics

CHAPTER 1

Politics

M.R.: Paradoxically, your political writings and your analyses of American imperialist ideology appear to be better known, in France as well as in the United States, than the new discipline which you have created: generative grammar. That poses the question: Do you see a link between your scientific activities—the study of language—and your political activities? For example, in the methods of analysis?

N.C.: If there is a connection, it is on a rather abstract level. I don't have access to any unusual methods of analysis, and what special knowledge I have concerning language has no immediate bearing on social and political issues. Everything I have written on these topics could have been written by someone else. There is no very direct connection between my political activities, writing and others, and the work bearing on language structure, though in some measure they perhaps derive from certain common assumptions and attitudes with regard to basic aspects of human nature. Critical analysis in the ideological arena seems to me to be a fairly straightforward matter as compared to an approach that requires a degree of conceptual abstraction. For the analysis of ideology, which occupies me very much, a bit of open-mindedness, normal intelligence, and healthy skepticism will generally suffice.

For example, take the question of the role of the intelligentsia in a society like ours. This social class, which includes historians and other scholars, journalists, political commentators, and so on, undertakes to analyze and present some picture of social reality. By virtue of their analyses and interpretations, they serve as mediators between the social facts and the mass of the population: they create the ideological justification for social practice. Look at the work of the specialists in contemporary affairs and compare their interpretation with the events, compare what they say with the world of fact. You will often find great and fairly systematic divergence. Then you can take a further step and try to explain these divergences, taking into account the class position of the intelligentsia.

Such analysis is, I think, of some importance, but the task is not very difficult, and the problems that arise do not seem to me to pose much of an intellectual challenge. With a little industry and application, anyone who is willing to extricate himself from the system of shared ideology and propaganda will readily see through the modes of distortion developed by substantial segments of the intelligentsia. Everybody is capable of doing that. If such analysis is often carried out poorly, that is because, quite commonly, social and political analysis is produced to defend special interests rather than to account for the actual events.

Precisely because of this tendency one must be careful not to give the impression, which in any event is false, that only intellectuals equipped with special training are capable of such analytic work. In fact that is just what the intelligentsia would often like us to think: they pretend to be engaged in an esoteric enterprise, inaccessible to simple people. But that's nonsense. The social sciences generally, and above all the analysis of contemporary affairs, are quite accessible to anyone who wants to take an interest in these matters. The alleged complexity, depth, and obscurity of these questions is part of the illusion propagated by the system of ideological control, which aims to make the issues seem remote from the general population and to persuade them of their incapacity to organize their own affairs or to understand the social world in which they live without the tutelage of intermediaries. For that reason alone one should be careful not to link the analysis of social issues with scientific topics which, for their part, do require special training and techniques, and thus a special intellectual frame of reference, before they can be seriously investigated.

In the analysis of social and political issues it is sufficient to face the facts and to be willing to follow a rational line of argument. Only Cartesian common sense, which is quite evenly distributed, is needed . . . if by that you understand the willingness to look at the facts with an open mind, to put simple assumptions to the test, and to pursue an argument to its conclusion. But beyond that no special esoteric knowledge is required to explore these "depths," which are nonexistent.

M.R.: In fact I'm thinking of the work which has been able to reveal the existence of "rules" of ideology, inaccessible to the consciousness of those caught up in history; for example, the study which Jean Pierre Faye has devoted to the rise of Nazism. This type of work shows that the critique of ideology can attain intellectual profundity.

N.C.: I do not say that it is impossible to create an intellectually interesting theory dealing with ideology and its social bases. That's possible, but it isn't necessary in order to understand, for example, what induces intellectuals often to disguise reality in the service of external power, or to see how it is done in particular cases of immediate importance. To be sure, one can treat all of this as an interesting topic of research. But we must separate two things:

1. Is it possible to present a significant theoretical analysis of this? Answer: Yes, in principle. And this type of work might attain a level at which it would require special training, and form, in principle, part of science.

2. Is such a science necessary to remove the distorting prism imposed by the intelligentsia on social reality? Answer: No. Ordinary skepticism and application is sufficient.

Let us take a concrete example: When an event occurs in the world, the mass media—television, the newspapers—look for someone to explain it. In the United States, at least, they turn to the professionals in social science, basing themselves on the notion, which seems superficially reasonable and in some instances is reasonable within limits, that these experts have a special competence to explain what is happening. Correspondingly, it is very important for the professionals to make everyone believe in the existence of an intellectual frame of reference which they alone possess, so that they alone have the right to comment on these affairs or are in a position to do so. This is one of the ways in which the professional intelligentsia serve a useful and effective function within the apparatus of social control. You don't ask the man in the street how to build a bridge, do you? You turn to a professional expert. Very well, in the same way you should not ask this man in the street: Must we intervene in Angola? Here one needs professionals—very carefully selected, to be sure.

To make all of this more concrete, let me comment in a very personal way: in my own professional work I have touched on a variety of different fields. I've done work in mathematical linguistics, for example, without any professional credentials in mathematics; in this subject I am completely self-taught, and not very well taught. But I've often been invited by universities to speak on mathematical linguistics at mathematics seminars and colloquia. No one has ever asked me whether I have the appropriate credentials to speak on these subjects; the mathematicians couldn't care less. What they want to know is what I have to say. No one has ever objected to my right to speak, asking whether I have a doctor's degree in mathematics, or whether I have taken advanced courses in this subject. That would never have entered their minds. They want to know whether I am right or wrong, whether the subject is interesting or not, whether better approaches are possible—the discussion dealt with the subject, not with my right to discuss it.

But on the other hand, in discussion or debate concerning social issues or American foreign policy, Vietnam or the Middle

East, for example, the issue is constantly raised, often with considerable venom. I've repeatedly been challenged on grounds of credentials, or asked, what special training do you have that entitles you to speak of these matters. The assumption is that people like me, who are outsiders from a professional viewpoint, are not entitled to speak on such things.

Compare mathematics and the political sciences—it's quite striking. In mathematics, in physics, people are concerned with what you say, not with your certification. But in order to speak about social reality, you must have the proper credentials, particularly if you depart from the accepted framework of thinking. Generally speaking, it seems fair to say that the richer the intellectual substance of a field, the less there is a concern for credentials, and the greater is the concern for content. One might even argue that to deal with substantive issues in the ideological disciplines may be a dangerous thing, because these disciplines are not simply concerned with discovering and explaining the facts as they are; rather, they tend to present these facts and interpret them in a manner that conforms to certain ideological requirements, and to become dangerous to established interests if they do not do so.

To complete the picture I should note a striking difference, in my personal experience at least, between the United States and other industrial democracies in this regard. Thus I have found over the years that although I am often asked to comment on international affairs or social issues by press, radio, and television in Canada, Western Europe, Japan, Australia, that is very rare in the United States.

(I exclude here the special pages of the newspapers in which a range of dissenting view is permitted, even encouraged, but encapsulated and identified as "full expression of a range of opinion." I am referring rather to the commentary and analysis that enters into the mainstream of discussion and interpretation of contemporary affairs, a crucial difference.)

The contrast was quite dramatic through the period of the Vietnam war, and remains so today. If this were solely a personal experience, it would not be of any significance, but I am quite sure it is not. The United States is unusual among the industrial democracies in the rigidity of the system of ideological control—"indoctrination," we might say—exercised through the mass media. One of the devices used to achieve this narrowness of perspective is the reliance on professional credentials. The universities and academic disciplines have, in the past, been successful in safeguarding conformist attitudes and interpretations, so that by and large a reliance on "professional expertise" will ensure that views and analyses that depart from orthodoxy will rarely be expressed.

Thus, when I hesitate to try to link my work in linguistics to analyses of current affairs or of ideology, as many people suggest, it is for two reasons. In the first place, the connection is in fact tenuous. Furthermore, I do not want to contribute to the illusion that these questions require technical understanding, inaccessible without special training. But I don't want to deny what you say: one can approach the nature of ideology, the role of ideological control, the social role of the intelligentsia, etc., in a sophisticated fashion. But the task which confronts the ordinary citizen concerned with understanding social reality and removing the masks that disguise it is not comparable to Jean Pierre Faye's problem in his investigation of totalitarian language.

M.R.:   In your analyses of ideology you have pointed to a "curious" fact: At times certain journals practice a policy of "balance," which consists of presenting contradictory reports or interpretations side by side. You said, however, that only the official version, that of the dominant ideology, was retained, even without proof, while the version of the opposition was rejected in spite of the evidence presented and the reliability of the sources.

N.C.:   Yes, in part because, obviously, privileged status is accorded to the version that conforms better to the needs of power and privilege. However, it is important not to overlook the tremendous imbalance as to how the social reality is presented to the public.

To my knowledge, in the American mass media you cannot find a single socialist journalist, not a single syndicated political commentator who is a socialist. From the ideological point of view the mass media are almost one hundred percent "state capitalist." In a sense, we have over here the "mirror image" of the Soviet Union, where all the people who write in *Pravda* represent the position which they call "socialism"—in fact, a certain variety of highly authoritarian state socialism. Here in the United States there is an astonishing degree of ideological uniformity for such a complex country. Not a single socialist voice in the mass media, not even a timid one; perhaps there are some marginal exceptions, but I cannot think of any, off-hand. Basically, there are two reasons for this. First, there is the remarkable ideological homogeneity of the American intelligentsia in general, who rarely depart from one of the variants of state capitalistic ideology (liberal or conservative), a fact which itself calls for explanation. The second reason is that the mass media are capitalist institutions. It is no doubt the same on the board of directors of General Motors. If no socialist is to be found on it—what would he be doing there!—it's not because they haven't been able to find anyone who is qualified. In a capitalist society the mass media are capitalist institutions. The fact that these institutions reflect the ideology of dominant economic interests is hardly surprising.

That is a crude and elementary fact. What you speak of points to more subtle phenomena. These, though interesting, must not make one forget the dominant factors.

It is notable that despite the extensive and well-known record of government lies during the period of the Vietnam war, the press, with fair consistency, remained remarkably obedient, and quite willing to accept the government's assumptions, framework of thinking, and interpretation of what was happening. Of course, on narrow technical questions—is the war succeeding? for example—the press was willing to criticize, and there were always honest correspondents in the field who described what they saw. But I am referring to the general pattern of interpretation and analysis, and to more general assumptions about what is right and proper. Furthermore, at times the press simply concealed easily documented facts—the bombing of Laos is a striking case.

But the subservience of the media is illustrated in less blatant ways as well. Take the peace treaty negotiations, revealed by Hanoi radio in October 1972, right before the November presidential elections. When Kissinger appeared on television to say that "peace is at hand," the press dutifully presented his version of what was happening, though even a cursory analysis of his comments showed that he was rejecting the basic principles of the negotiations on every crucial point, so that further escalation of the American war—as in fact took place with the Christmas bombings—was inevitable. I do not say this only with the benefit of hindsight. I and others exerted considerable energy trying to get the national press to face the obvious facts at the time, and I also wrote an article about it before the Christmas bombings,[1] which in particular predicted "increased terror bombing of North Vietnam."

The exact same story was replayed in January 1973, when the peace treaty was finally announced. Again Kissinger and the White House made it clear that the United States was rejecting every basic principle in the treaty it was signing, so that continued war was inevitable. The press dutifully accepted the official version, and even allowed some amazing falsehoods to stand unchallenged. I've discussed all of this in detail elsewhere.[2]

Or to mention another case, in an article written for *Ramparts,*[3] I reviewed the retrospective interpretations of the war in Vietnam presented in the press when the war came to an end in 1975—the liberal press, the rest is not interesting in this connection.

Virtually without exception, the press accepted the basic principles of government propaganda, without questioning them. Here we're talking about that part of the press which considered itself as opposed to the war. That's very striking.

The same is often true of passionate critics of the war; presumably, to a large extent they aren't even conscious of it.

That applies particularly to those who are sometimes considered the "intellectual élite." There is, in fact, a curious book called *The American Intellectual Elite* by C. Kadushin, which presents the results of an elaborate opinion survey of a group identified as "the intellectual élite," undertaken in 1970. This book contains a great deal of information on the group's attitudes toward the war at the time when opposition to the war was at its peak. The overwhelming majority considered themselves to be opponents of the war, but in general for what they called "pragmatic" reasons: they became convinced at a given moment that the United States could not win at an acceptable cost. I imagine a study of the "German intellectual élite" in 1944 would have produced similar results. The study indicates quite dramatically the remarkable degree of conformity and submission to the dominant ideology among people who considered themselves informed critics of government policy.

The consequence of this conformist subservience to those in power, as Hans Morgenthau correctly termed it, is that in the United States political discourse and debate has often been less diversified even than in certain Fascist countries, Franco Spain, for example, where there was lively discussion covering a broad ideological range. Though the penalties for deviance from official doctrine were incomparably more severe than here, nevertheless opinion and thinking was not constrained within such narrow limits, a fact that frequently occasioned surprise among Spanish intellectuals visiting the United States during the latter years of the Franco period. Much the same was true in Fascist Portugal, where there seem to have been significant Marxist groups in the universities, to mention just one example. The range and significance of the ideological diversity became apparent with the fall of the dictatorship, and is also reflected in the liberation movements in the Portuguese colonies—a two-way street, in that case, in that the Portuguese intellectuals were influenced by the liberation movements, and conversely, I suppose.

In the United States the situation is quite different. As compared with the other capitalist democracies, the United States is considerably more rigid and doctrinaire in its political thinking and analysis. Not only among the intelligentsia, though in this sector the fact is perhaps most striking. The United States is exceptional also in that there is no significant pressure for worker participation in management, let alone real workers' control. These issues are not alive in the United States, as they are throughout Western Europe. And the absence of any significant socialist voice or discussion is again quite a striking feature of the United States, as compared to other societies of comparable social structure and level of economic development.

Here one saw some small changes at the end of the sixties; but in 1965 you would have had great difficulty in finding a Marxist professor, or a socialist, in an economics department at a major university, for example. State capitalist ideology dominated the social sciences and every ideological discipline almost entirely. This conformism was called "the end of ideology." It dominated the professional fields—and still largely does—as well as the mass media and the journals of opinion. Such a degree of ideological conformity in a country which does not have a secret police, at least not much of one, and does not have concentration camps, is quite remarkable. Here the range of ideological diversity (the kind that implies lively debate on social issues) for many years has been very narrow, skewed much more to the right than in other industrial democracies. This is important. The subtleties to which you alluded must be considered within this framework.

Some changes did take place at the end of the sixties in the universities, largely due to the student movement, which demanded and achieved some broadening of the tolerated range of thinking. The reactions have been interesting. Now that the pressure of the student movement has been reduced, there is a substantial effort to reconstruct the orthodoxy that had been slightly disturbed. And constantly, in the discussions and the literature dealing with that period—often called "the time of troubles" or something of that sort—the student left is depicted as a menace threatening freedom of research and teaching; the student movement is said to have placed the freedom of the universities in jeopardy by seeking to impose totalitarian ideological controls. That is how the state capitalist intellectuals describe the fact that their near-total control of ideology was very briefly brought into question, as they seek to close again these slight breaches in the system of thought control, and to reverse the process through which just a little diversity arose within the ideological institutions: the totalitarian menace of fascism of the left! And they really believe this, to such an extent have they been brainwashed and controlled by their own ideological commitments. One expects that from the police, but when it comes from the intellectuals, then that's very striking.

It is certainly true that there were some cases in the American universities when the actions of the students went beyond the limits of what is proper and legitimate. Some of the worst incidents, as we know now, were instigated by government provocateurs,[4] though a few, without doubt, represented excesses of the student movement itself. Those are the incidents on which many commentators focus their attention when they condemn the student movement.

The major effect of the student movement, however, was quite different, I believe. It raised a challenge to the subservience of the universities to the state and other external powers —although that challenge has not proven very effective, and this subordination has remained largely intact—and it managed to provoke, at times with some limited success, an opening in the ideological fields, thus bringing a slightly greater diversity of thought and study and research. In my opinion, it was this challenge to ideological control, mounted by the students (most of them liberals), chiefly in the social sciences, which induced such terror, verging at times on hysteria, in the reactions of the "intellectual élite." The analytic and retrospective studies which appear today often seem to me highly exaggerated and inexact in their account of the events that took place and their significance. Many intellectuals are seeking to reconstruct the orthodoxy and the control over thought and inquiry which they had institutionalized with such success, and which was in fact threatened—freedom is always a threat to the commissars.

M.R.:   The student movement was first mobilized against the war in Vietnam, but did it not quite soon involve other issues?

N.C.:   The immediate issue was the Vietnam war, but also the civil rights movement of the preceding years—you must remember that the activists in the vanguard of the civil rights movement in the South had very often been students, for example, SNCC (Student Non-violent Coordinating Committee), which was a very important and effective group with a largely black leadership, and supported by many white students. Furthermore, some of the earlier issues had to do with opening up the campus to a greater range of thought and to political activity of diverse tendencies, as in the Berkeley free speech controversy.

It did not seem to me at the time that the student activists were really trying to "politicize" the universities. During the period when the domination of faculty ideologues was not yet at issue, the universities were highly politicized and made regular and significant contributions to external powers, especially to the government, its programs and its policies; this continued to be true during the period of the student movement, just as it is today. It would be more exact to say that the student movement, from the beginning, tried to open up the universities and free them from outside control. To be sure, from the point of view of those who had subverted the universities and converted them to a significant extent into instruments of government policy and official ideology this effort appeared to be an illegitimate form of "politicization." All of this seems obvious as regards university laboratories devoted to weapons production or social science programs with intimate connections to counterinsurgency, government intelligence services and propaganda, and social control. It is less obvious, perhaps, but nevertheless true, I think, in the domain of academic scholarship.

To illustrate this, take the example of the history of the cold war, and the so-called revisionist interpretation of the period following World War II. The "revisionists," as you know, were those American commentators who opposed the official "orthodox" version. This orthodoxy, quite dominant at the time, held that the cold war was due solely to Russian and Chinese aggressiveness, and that the United States played a passive role, merely reacting to this. This position was adopted by even the most liberal commentators. Take a man like John Kenneth Galbraith, who within the liberal establishment has long been one of the most open, questioning, and skeptical minds, one of those who tried to break out of the orthodox framework on many issues. Well, in his book *The New Industrial State,* published in 1967—as late as that!—where he lays much stress on the open and critical attitude of the intelligentsia and the encouraging prospects this offers, he says that "the undoubted historical source" of the cold war was Russian and Chinese aggressiveness: "the revolutionary and national aspirations of the Soviets, and more recently of the Chinese, and the compulsive vigor of their assertion."[5] That is what the liberal critics were still saying in 1967.

The "revisionist" alternative was developed in various conflicting versions by James Warburg, D. F. Fleming, William Appleman Williams, Gar Alperovitz, Gabriel Kolko, David Horowitz, Diane Clemens, and others. They argued that the cold war resulted from an interaction of great power designs and suspicions. This position not only has prima facie plausibility, but also receives strong support from the historical and documentary record. But few people paid much attention to "revisionist" studies, which were often the object of scorn or a few pleasantries among "serious" analysts.

By the end of the sixties, however, it had become impossible to prevent serious consideration of the "revisionist" position, in large part because of the pressures of the student movement. Students had read these books and wanted to have them discussed. What resulted is quite interesting.

In the first place, as soon as the revisionist alternative was seriously considered, the orthodox position simply dissolved, vanished. As soon as the debate was opened, it found itself lacking an object, virtually. The orthodox position was abandoned.

To be sure, orthodox historians rarely admitted that they had been in error. Instead, while adopting some of the revisionist views, they attributed to the revisionists a stupid position, according to which—to take a not untypical characterization— "the Soviet Government . . . was merely the hapless object of our vicious diplomacy." This is Herbert Feis's rendition of the position of Gar Alperovitz, whose actual view was that "the Cold War cannot be understood simply as an American response to a Soviet challenge, but rather as the insidious interaction of mutual suspicions, blame for which must be shared by all." Quite typically, the view attributed to the revisionists was a nonsensical one that takes no account of interaction of the superpowers. Orthodox historians took over some elements of the revisionist analysis, while attributing to them an idiotic doctrine that was fundamentally different from what had actually been proposed, and in fact was the mirror image of the original orthodox position. The motivation for this mode of argument is of course obvious enough.

Starting from this slightly revised basis, many orthodox historians have sought to reconstruct the image of American benevolence and passivity. But I do not want to go into this development here. As for the impact of the revisionist analysis, Galbraith again provides an interesting example: I have already quoted his book, which appeared in 1967. In a revised edition, in 1971, he replaced the word "the" by the word "an" in the passage quoted: "the revolutionary and national aspirations of the Soviets, and more recently of the Chinese, and the compulsive vigor of their assertion, were *an* undoubted historical source [of the cold war]" (my emphasis). This account is still misleading and biased, because he does not speak of the *other* causes; it would also be interesting to see in just what way the initiatives of China were "an undoubted source" of the cold war. But the position is at least tenable, in contrast to the orthodox position, which he gave in the previous edition four years earlier—and prior to the general impact of the student movement on the universities.

Galbraith is an interesting example just because he is one of the most open, critical, and questioning minds among the liberal intelligentsia. His comments on the cold war and its origins are also interesting because they are presented as a casual side remark: he does not attempt in this context to give an original historical analysis, but merely reports in passing the doctrine accepted among those liberal intellectuals who were somewhat skeptical and critical. We are not talking here about an Arthur Schlesinger or other ideologues who at times present a selection of historical facts in a manner comparable to the party historians of other faiths.

One can understand why so many liberal intellectuals were terrified at the end of the sixties, why they describe this period as one of totalitarianism of the left: for once they were compelled to look the world of facts in the face. A serious threat, and a real danger for people whose role is ideological control. There is a recent and quite interesting study put out by the Trilateral Commission—*The Crisis of Democracy,* by Michel Crozier, Samuel Huntington, and Joji Watanuki—in which an international group of scholars and others discuss what they see as contemporary threats to democracy. One of these threats is posed by "value-oriented intellectuals" who, as they correctly point out, often challenge the institutions that are responsible for "the indoctrination of the young"—an apt phrase. The student movement contributed materially to this aspect of "the crisis of democracy."

By the late sixties the discussion had gone beyond the question of Vietnam or the interpretation of contemporary history; it concerned the *institutions* themselves. Orthodox economics was very briefly challenged by students who wanted to undertake a fundamental critique of the functioning of the capitalist economy; students questioned the institutions, they wanted to study Marx and political economy.

Perhaps I can illustrate this once again with a personal anecdote:

In the spring of 1969 a small group of students in economics here in Cambridge wanted to initiate a discussion of the nature of economics as a field of study. In order to open this discussion, they tried to organize a debate in which the two main speakers would be Paul Samuelson, the eminent Keynesian economist at MIT (today a Nobel laureate), and a Marxist economist. But for this latter role they were not able to find anyone in the Boston area, no one who was willing to question the neo-classical position from the point of view of Marxist political economy. Finally I was asked to take on the task, though I have no particular knowledge of economics, and no commitment to Marxism. Not one professional, or even semi-professional, in 1969! And Cambridge is a very lively place in these respects. That may give you some idea of the prevailing intellectual climate. It is difficult to imagine anything comparable in Western Europe or Japan.

The student movement changed these things to a small extent: what was described, as I told you, as terror at the university . . . the SS marching through the corridors . . . the academic intelligentsia barely survived these terrifying attacks by student radicals . . . of course, due solely to their great courage. Unbelievable fantasies! Although, to be sure, there were incidents, sometimes instigated by provocateurs of the FBI, as we know now, which stimulated that paranoid interpretation. What a devastating thing, to have opened up the university just a little! But the mass media were hardly touched at all, and now orthodoxy has been reestablished, because the pressure is no longer there. For example, a serious diplomatic historian like Gaddis Smith can now describe Williams and Kolko as "pamphleteers" in the *New York Times Book Review*.

M.R.: To what do you attribute this "falling off" of the pressure?

N.C.: To many things. When the New Left developed within the student movement in the United States, it could not associate itself with any broader social movement, rooted in any important segment of the population. In large part this was the result of the ideological narrowness of the preceding period. Students form a social group that is marginal and transitory. The student left constituted a small minority, often confronted by very difficult circumstances. A living intellectual tradition of the left did not exist, nor a socialist movement with a base in the working class. There was no living tradition or popular movement from which they could gain support. Under these circumstances, it is perhaps surprising that the student movement lasted as long as it did.

M.R.: And the new generation?

N.C.: It is faced with new forms of experience. Students today seem to find it easier to adapt to the demands imposed from the outside, though one should not exaggerate; in my experience at least, colleges are quite unlike the fifties and early sixties. The economic stagnation and recession have a lot to do with student attitudes. Under the conditions of the sixties students could suppose that they would find means of subsistence, no matter what they did. The society seemed to have sufficient interstices, there was a sense of expansiveness and optimism, so that one could hope to find a place somehow. Now that is no longer the case. Even those who are "disciplined" and well prepared professionally may become well-educated taxi drivers. Student activism has felt the effect of all this.

Other factors have also played a role. There is evidence that certain universities, perhaps many of them, have explicitly sought to exclude leftist students. Even in liberal universities, political criteria have been imposed to exclude students who might "cause problems." Not entirely, of course, otherwise they would have excluded all the good students. Leftist students also have had serious difficulties in working at the universities, or later, in gaining appointments, at least in the ideological disciplines, political science, economics, Asian studies, for example.

M.R.:   At the time of the French publication of your book *Counterrevolutionary Violence (Bains de Sang)* there was much talk in France about the fact that the English original had been censored (that is, distribution was blocked) by the conglomerate to which the publishing house belonged; the publishing house itself was closed and its personnel dismissed. The chief editor became a taxi driver and now is organizing a taxi-drivers' union. French television has cast doubt on this story.

N.C.:   That "censorship" by the conglomerate did take place, as you describe, but it was a stupid act on their part. At that level censorship isn't necessary, given the number of potential readers on the one hand, and on the other, the weight exerted by the enormous ideological apparatus. I have often thought that if a rational Fascist dictatorship were to exist, then it would choose the American system. State censorship is not necessary, or even very efficient, in comparison to the ideological controls exercised by systems that are more complex and more decentralized.

M.R.:   Within this framework, how do you interpret the Watergate affair, which has often been presented in France as the "triumph" of democracy?

N.C.:   To consider the Watergate affair as a triumph of democracy is an error, in my opinion. The real question raised was not: Did Nixon employ evil methods against his political adversaries? but rather: Who were the victims? The answer is clear. Nixon was condemned, not because he employed reprehensible methods in his political struggles, but because he made a mistake in the choice of adversaries against whom he turned these methods. *He attacked people with power.*

The telephone taps? Such practices have existed for a long time. He had an "enemies list"? But nothing happened to those who were on that list. I was on that list, nothing happened to me. No, he simply made a mistake in his choice of enemies: he had on his list the chairman of IBM, senior government advisers, distinguished pundits of the press, highly placed supporters of the Democratic Party. He attacked the Washington *Post,* a major capitalist enterprise. And these powerful people defended themselves at once, as would be expected. Watergate? Men of power against men of power.

Similar crimes, and others much graver, could have been charged against other people as well as Nixon. But those crimes were typically directed against minorities or against movements of social change, and few ever protested. The ideological censorship kept these matters from the public eye during the Watergate period, although remarkable documentation concerning this repression appeared at just this time. It was only when the dust of Watergate had settled that the press and the political commentators turned toward some of the real and profound cases of abuse of state power—still without recognizing or exploring the gravity of the issue.

For example, the Church Committee has published information, the significance of which has not really been made clear. At the time of its revelations, a great deal of publicity was focused on the Martin Luther King affair, but still more important revelations have hardly been dealt with by the press to this day (January 1976). For example, the following: In Chicago there was a street gang called the Blackstone Rangers, which operated in the ghetto. The Black Panthers were in contact with them, attempting to politicize them, it appears. As long as the Rangers remained a ghetto street gang—a criminal gang, as depicted by the FBI, at least—the FBI were not much concerned; this was also a way of controlling the ghetto. But radicalized into a political group, they became potentially dangerous.

The basic function of the FBI is not to stop crime. Rather, it functions as a political police, in large measure. An indication is given by the FBI budget and the way it is apportioned. Some suggestive information on this subject has been revealed by a group calling themselves the "Citizens' Commission to Investigate the FBI," who succeeded in stealing from the FBI's Media, Pennsylvania, office a collection of documents which they attempted to circulate to the press. The breakdown of these documents was approximately the following: 30 percent were devoted to routine procedures; 40 percent to political surveillance involving two right-wing groups, ten groups concerned with immigrants, and more than two hundred liberal or left-wing groups; 14 percent to AWOLs and deserters; 1 percent to organized crime—mostly gambling—and the rest to rape, bank robbery, murder, etc.

Faced with the potential alliance of the Rangers and the Black Panthers, the FBI decided to take action, in line with the national program of dismantling the left in which it was engaged, the national Counter-Intelligence Program known as Cointelpro. They sought to incite conflict between the two groups by means of a forgery, an anonymous letter sent to the leader of the Rangers by someone who identified himself as "a black brother." This letter warned of a Panther plot to assassinate the leader of the Rangers. Its transparent purpose was to incite the Rangers—described in FBI documents as a group "to whom violent type activity, shooting, and the like, are second nature"—to respond with violence to the fictitious assassination plot.

But it didn't work, perhaps because at that time the relations between the Rangers and the Panthers were already too close. The FBI had to take on the task of destroying the Panthers itself. How?

Though there has been no systematic investigation, we can reconstruct what seems to be a plausible story:

A few months later, in December 1969, the Chicago police conducted a pre-dawn raid on a Panther apartment. Approximately one hundred shots were fired. At first the police claimed that they had responded to the fire of the Panthers, but it was quickly established by the local press that this was false. Fred Hampton, one of the most talented and promising leaders of the Panthers, was killed in his bed. There is evidence that he may have been drugged. Witnesses claim that he was murdered in cold blood. Mark Clark was also killed. This event can fairly be described as a Gestapo-style political assassination.

At the time it was thought that the Chicago police were behind the raid. That would have been bad enough, but the facts revealed since suggest something more sinister. We know today that Hampton's personal bodyguard, William O'Neal, who was also chief of Panther security, was an FBI infiltrator. A few days before the raid, the FBI office turned over to the Chicago police a floor plan of the Panther apartment supplied by O'Neal, with the location of the beds marked, along with a rather dubious report by O'Neal that illegal weapons were kept in the apartment: the pretext for the raid. Perhaps the floor plan explains the fact, noticed by reporters, that the police gunfire was directed to inside corners of the apartment rather than the entrances. It certainly undermines still further the original pretense that the police were firing in response to Panther gunshots, confused by unfamiliar surroundings. The Chicago press has reported that the FBI agent to whom O'Neal reported was the head of Chicago Cointelpro directed against the Black Panthers and other black groups. Whether or not this is true, there is direct evidence of FBI complicity in the murders.

Putting this information together with the documented effort of the FBI to incite violence and gang warfare a few months earlier, it seems not unreasonable to speculate that the FBI undertook on its own initiative the murder that it could not elicit from the "violence-prone" group to which it had addressed a fabricated letter implicating the Panthers in an assassination attempt against its leader.

This one incident (which, incidentally, was not seriously investigated by the Church Committee) completely overshadows the entire Watergate episode in significance by a substantial margin. But with a few exceptions the national press or television have had little to say on the subject, though it has been well covered locally in Chicago. The matter has rarely been dealt with by political commentators. The comparison with coverage of such "atrocities" as Nixon's "enemies list" or tax trickery is quite striking. For example, during the entire Watergate period, the *New Republic,* which was then virtually the official organ of American liberalism, found no occasion to report or comment on these matters, although the basic facts and documents had become known.

The family of Fred Hampton brought a civil suit against the Chicago police, but up to the present the FBI involvement has been excluded from the courts, although much relevant information is available in depositions made under oath.

If people offended by "Watergate horrors" were really concerned with civil and human rights, they should have pursued the information released by the Church Committee with regard to the affair of the Blackstone Rangers, and considered the possible relevance of this information to what is known concerning FBI involvement in the murder of Fred Hampton by the Chicago police. At least a serious inquiry should have been initiated to examine what seem to be possible connections, and to bring to light the FBI role under Nixon and his predecessors. For what was at issue here was an assassination in which the national political police may have been implicated, a crime that far transcends anything attributed to Nixon in the Watergate investigations. I should recall that the Watergate inquiry did touch on one issue of extraordinary importance, the bombing of Cambodia, but only on very narrow grounds—it was the alleged "secrecy" of the bombings, not the fact itself, that was charged to Nixon as his "crime" in this regard.

There are other cases of this kind. For example, in San Diego the FBI apparently financed, armed, and controlled an extreme right-wing group of former Minute Men, transforming it into something called the Secret Army Organization specializing in terrorist acts of various kinds. I heard of this first from one of my former students, who was the target of an assassination attempt by the organization. In fact, he is the student who had organized the debate on economics that I told you about a little while ago, when he was still a student at MIT. Now he was teaching at San Diego State College and was engaged in political activities—which incidentally were completely nonviolent, not that this is relevant.

The head of the Secret Army Organization—a provocateur in the pay of the FBI—drove past his house, and his companion fired shots into it, seriously wounding a young woman. The young man who was their target was not at home at the time. The weapon had been stolen by this FBI provocateur. According to the local branch of the ACLU, the gun was handed over the next day to the San Diego FBI Bureau, who hid it; and for six months the FBI lied to the San Diego police about the incident. This affair did not become publicly known until later.

This terrorist group, directed and financed by the FBI, was finally broken up by the San Diego police, after they had tried to fire-bomb a theater in the presence of police. The FBI agent in question, who had hidden the weapon, was transferred outside the state of California so that he could not be prosecuted. The FBI provocateur also escaped prosecution, though several members of the secret terrorist organization were prosecuted. The FBI was engaged in efforts to incite gang warfare among black groups in San Diego, as in Chicago, at about the same time. In secret documents, the FBI took credit for inciting shootings, beatings, and unrest in the ghetto, a fact that has elicited very little comment in the press or journals of opinion.

This same young man, incidentally, was harassed in other ways. It appears that the FBI continued to subject him to various kinds of intimidation and threats, by means of provocateurs. Furthermore, according to his ACLU attorneys, the FBI supplied information to the college where he was teaching that was the basis for misconduct charges filed against him. He faced three successive inquiries at the college, and each time was absolved of the charges brought against him. At that point the chancellor of the California state college system, Glenn Dumke, stated that he would not accept the findings of the independent hearing committees and simply dismissed him from his position. Notice that such incidents, of which there have been a fair number, are not regarded as "totalitarianism" in the university.

The basic facts were submitted to the Church Committee by the ACLU in June 1975 and also offered to the press. As far as I know, the committee did not conduct any investigation into the matter. The national press said virtually nothing about these incidents at the time, and very little since.

There have been similar reports concerning other government programs of repression. For example, Army Intelligence has been reported to have engaged in illegal actions in Chicago. In Seattle, fairly extensive efforts were undertaken to disrupt and discredit local left-wing groups. The FBI ordered one of its agents to induce a group of young radicals to blow up a bridge; this was to be done in such a manner that the person who was to plant the bomb would also be blown up with it. The agent refused to carry out these instructions. Instead, he talked to the press and finally testified in court. That is how the matter became known. In Seattle FBI infiltrators were inciting arson, terrorism, and bombing, and in one case entrapped a young black man in a robbery attempt, which they initiated and in the course of which he was killed. This was reported by Frank Donner in the *Nation,* one of the few American journals to have attempted some serious coverage of such matters.

There is a good deal more of this. But all these isolated cases only take on their full meaning if you put them into the context of the policies of the FBI since its origins during the post–World War I Red scare, which I will not try to review here. The Cointelpro operations began in the 1950s, with a program to disrupt and destroy the Communist Party. Although this was not officially proclaimed, everybody knew something of the sort was going on, and there were very few protests; it was considered quite legitimate. People even joked about it.

In 1960 the disruption program was extended to the Puerto Rican independence movement. In October 1961, under the administration of Attorney-General Robert Kennedy, the FBI initiated a disruption program against the Socialist Workers Party (the largest Trotskyist organization); the program was later extended to the civil rights movement, the Ku Klux Klan, black nationalist groups, and the peace movement in general; by 1968 it covered the entire "New Left."

The rationale given internally for these illegal programs is quite revealing. The program for disrupting the Socialist Workers Party, which came directly from the central office of the FBI, presented its rationale in essentially these terms:

> We launch this program for the following reasons:
> (1) the Socialist Workers Party is openly running candidates in local elections throughout the country;
> (2) it supports integration in the South;
> (3) it supports Castro.

What does this actually indicate? It means that SWP political initiative in running candidates in elections—*legal* political activity—their work in support of civil rights, and their efforts to change U.S. foreign policy justify their destruction at the hands of the national political police.

This is the rationale behind these programs of government repression: they were directed against civil rights activities and against legal political action that ran counter to the prevailing consensus. In comparison with Cointelpro and related government actions in the 1960s, Watergate was a tea party. It is instructive, however, to compare the relative attention accorded to them in the press. This comparison reveals clearly and dramatically that it was the improper choice of targets, not improper acts, that led to Nixon's downfall. The alleged concern for civil and democratic rights was a sham. There was no "triumph of democracy."

M.R.:   It appears that a proposal, containing passages from the Constitution of the United States and the Bill of Rights, was distributed in the streets at one time and people refused to sign them, believing them to be left-wing propaganda.

N.C.:   Such incidents have been reported from the 1950s, if I recall. People have been intimidated for many years. Liberals would like to believe that all of this is due to a few evil men: Joe McCarthy and Richard Nixon. That is quite false. One can trace the postwar repression to security measures initiated by Truman in 1947, and efforts by Democratic liberals to discredit Henry Wallace and his supporters at that time. It was the liberal senator Hubert Humphrey who proposed detention camps in case of a "national emergency." He did finally vote against the McCarran Act, but said at the time that he found it not sufficiently harsh in some respects; he was opposed to the provision that prisoners in the detention camps should be protected by the right of habeas corpus: that was not the way to treat Communist conspirators! The Communist Control Act introduced by leading liberals a few years later was so patently unconstitutional that no one actually tried to enforce it, to my knowledge. This law, incidentally, was specifically directed in part against trade unions. And together with these senators, many liberal intellectuals implicitly supported the fundamental aims of "McCarthyism," though they objected to his methods —particularly when they too became targets. They carried out what amounted to a partial "purge" in the universities, and in many ways developed the ideological framework for ridding American society of this "cancer" of serious dissent. These are among the reasons for the remarkable conformism and ideological narrowness of intellectual life in the United States, and for the isolation of the student movement that we discussed earlier.

If these liberals opposed McCarthy, it was because he went too far, and in the wrong way. He attacked the liberal intelligentsia themselves, or mainstream political figures like George Marshall, instead of confining himself to the "Communist enemy." Like Nixon, he made a mistake in choosing his enemies when he began to attack the Church and the Army. Commonly, if liberal intellectuals criticized him, it was on the grounds that his methods were not the right ones for ridding the country of real communists. There were some notable exceptions, but depressingly few.

Similarly, Justice Robert Jackson, one of the leading liberals on the Supreme Court, opposed the doctrine of "clear and present danger" (according to which freedom of speech could be abridged in cases affecting the security of the state) when applied to Communist activities, because it was not harsh enough. If you wait until the danger becomes "clear and present," he explained, it will be too late. You must stop Communists *before* their "imminent actions." Thus he supported a truly totalitarian point of view: We must not permit this kind of discussion to begin.

But these liberals were very shocked when McCarthy turned his weapons against them. He was no longer playing according to the rules of the game—the game that they invented.

M.R.: Similarly, I've noticed that the scandal involving the CIA did not concern the main activities of the agency, but the fact that it did work which in principle was the assigned sphere of the FBI.

N.C.: In part, yes. And look at the furor that has arisen over the attempts at political assassination organized by the CIA. People were shocked because the CIA tried to assassinate foreign leaders. Certainly, that is very bad. But these were only abortive attempts; at least in most cases—in some it is not so clear. Consider in comparison the Phoenix program in which the CIA was involved, which, according to the Saigon government, exterminated forty thousand civilians within two years. Why doesn't that count? Why are all these people less significant than Castro or Schneider or Lumumba?

The official who was responsible for this, William Colby, who headed the CIA, is now a respected columnist and lecturer on university campuses. The same thing happened in Laos, though even worse. How many peasants were killed as a result of CIA programs? And who speaks of this? Nobody. No headlines.

It's always the same story. The crimes that are exposed are significant, but they are trivial as compared to the really serious criminal programs of the state, which are ignored or regarded as quite legitimate.

M.R.:   How do you find all this information? If the newspapers don't report it . . .

N.C.:   This information is accessible, but only for *fanatics:* in order to unearth it, you have to devote much of your life to the search. In that sense the information is accessible. But this "accessibility" is hardly significant in practice. It is politically more or less irrelevant. All the same, on the personal level, the situation for someone like me is of course incomparably preferable in the United States to the totalitarian societies. In the Soviet Union, for example, someone who tried to do what I do here would probably be in prison. It is interesting, and typical, that my political writings critical of U.S. policies are never translated in the so-called Communist countries, though they are, quite widely, in many other parts of the world. But one must be cautious in assessing the political significance of the relative freedom from repression—at least for the privileged— in the United States. Exactly what does it mean, concretely?

For example, last year I was invited to give a lecture at Harvard before a group of journalists called the Nieman Fellows, who come there each year from all over the United States and foreign countries in order to further their education, so to speak. They asked me to discuss Watergate and related topics —the press generally was quite proud of its courageous and principled behavior during the Watergate period, for very little reason, as I've just tried to explain. Instead of discussing Watergate, I spoke about the things to which I've just alluded, because I wondered to what extent these journalists, who are quite sophisticated and well informed compared to the general population, might know about these matters. Well, none of them had any idea of the scale of the FBI programs of repression, except for one journalist from Chicago, who knew all about the Hampton affair. That had indeed been discussed in detail in the Chicago press. If there had been someone from San Diego in the group, he would have known about the Secret Army Organization, and so forth . . .

That is one of the keys to the whole thing. Everyone is led to think that what he knows represents a local exception. *But the overall pattern remains hidden.* Information is often given in the local papers, but its general significance, the patterns on the national level, remain obscured. That was the case during the entire Watergate period, although the information appeared just at that time, in its essentials, and with extensive documentation. And even since then the discussion has rarely been analytic or anywhere near comprehensive, and has not accounted for what happened in a satisfactory manner. What you face here is a very effective kind of ideological control, because one can remain under the impression that censorship does not exist, and in a narrow technical sense that is correct. You will not be imprisoned if you discover the facts, not even if you proclaim them whenever you can. But the results remain much the same as if there were real censorship. Social reality is generally concealed by the intelligentsia. Of course matters were quite different during the period when there was an enormous popular anti-war and student movement. Within the structure of popular movements there were many possibilities for expressing views that departed from the narrow limits of more or less "official" ideology, to which the intelligentsia generally conform.

M.R.: What was the reaction of Americans to the statements of Solzhenitsyn?

N.C.: Very interesting—at least in the liberal press, which is what primarily concerns me. Some criticized his extravagances. He went well beyond what they could tolerate. For example, he called for direct intervention by the United States in the USSR—of a sort that could very well lead to war and, far short of that, is likely to harm the Russian dissidents themselves. Also, he denounced American weakness in abandoning the struggle to subdue the Vietnamese resistance, publicly opposed democratic reforms in Spain, supported a journal that called for censorship in the United States, and so on. Nonetheless, the press never ceased marveling at what an absolute moral giant this man was. In our petty lives, we can barely imagine such heights of moral grandeur.

In fact, the "moral level" of Solzhenitsyn is quite comparable to that of many American Communists who have fought courageously for civil liberties here in their own country, while at the same time defending, or refusing to criticize, the purges and labor camps in the Soviet Union. Sakharov is not as outlandish in his views as Solzhenitsyn, certainly, but he too says that it was a great setback for the West not to have pursued the Vietnam war to an American victory. The United States did not act with sufficient resolution, and delayed too long in sending a large expeditionary force, he complains. Every fabrication of the U.S. propaganda apparatus is repeated, just as American Communists who have struggled for civil rights here parrot Russian propaganda. The easily documented fact of American aggression in South Vietnam is not part of history, for example. One must admire Sakharov's great courage and his fine work in defense of human rights in the Soviet Union. But to refer to such people as "moral giants" is quite remarkable.

Why do they do this? Because it is extremely important for mainstream American intellectuals to make people believe that the United States does not confront any real moral problems. Such problems only arise in the Soviet Union, and the "moral giants" are there to respond to them.

Compare Solzhenitsyn to many thousands of Vietnam war resisters and deserters; many of them acted at a moral level that is incomparably superior to his. Solzhenitsyn resolutely defends his own rights and those of people like him—which is certainly admirable. The resisters and many deserters defended the *rights of others*—namely, the victims of American aggression and terror. Their actions were on a much higher moral plane. Furthermore, their actions were not merely a response to their own persecution; for the most part they undertook these actions, which led to imprisonment or exile, of their own free will, when they could have easily lived in comfort. Yet we read in the American liberal journals that we can hardly conceive of the moral grandeur of Solzhenitsyn in our society, and surely can find no one like him. A very interesting pretense, with many implications.

It is quite generally claimed now that the American resistance had as its cause the young men's fear of being drafted; that's a very convenient belief for the intellectuals who confined themselves to "pragmatic" opposition to the war. But it is an enormous lie. For most of those who were in the resistance from its origins, nothing would have been easier than to escape the draft, with its class bias, as many others actually did. In fact, many of the activists already had deferments. Many of the deserters too chose a difficult and painful course for reasons of principle. But for those who supported the war initially, and who only raised their whisper of protest when the costs became too great, it is impossible to admit the existence of a courageous and principled resistance, largely on the part of youth, to the atrocities which they themselves had readily tolerated. The mainstream of American liberalism does not wish to hear anything about all that. It would raise too many embarrassing questions: What were they doing when the war resisters were facing prison or exile? And so on. So Solzhenitsyn comes to them as a gift of God, which permits them to evade moral questions, "exporting them," so to speak, and to conceal their own role as people who remained silent for so many years, or finally objected on narrow and morally repugnant grounds of cost and U.S. government interest.

Moynihan, when he was ambassador to the United Nations, produced the same effect when he attacked the Third World.

These attacks aroused great admiration here; for example, when he denounced Idi Amin of Uganda as a "racist murderer." The question is not whether Idi Amin is a racist murderer. No doubt the appelation is correct. The question is, what does it mean for Moynihan to make this accusation and for others to applaud his honesty and courage in doing so? Who is Moynihan? He served in four administrations, those of Kennedy, Johnson, Nixon, and Ford—that is to say, administrations that were guilty of racist murder on a scale undreamed of by Idi Amin. Imagine that some minor functionary of the Third Reich had correctly accused someone of being a racist murderer. This manner of shifting moral issues to others is one of the ways to reconstruct the foundations of moral legitimacy for the exercise of American power, shaken during the Vietnam war. Solzhenitsyn is exploited to this end in a natural and predictable way, though of course one cannot on those grounds draw any conclusions in regard to his charges against the Soviet system of oppression and violence.

Think of someone like Angela Davis: she defends the rights of American blacks with great courage and conviction. At the same time she refused to defend Czech dissidents or to criticize the Russian invasion of Czechoslovakia. Is she regarded as a "moral giant"? Hardly. Yet I believe she is superior to Solzhenitsyn on the moral level. At least she did not reproach the Soviet Union for not having conducted its atrocities with sufficient vigor.

M.R.:   After what you have said, and what is said about the U.S. intervention in Chile in Uribe's book,[6] there apparently exists a veritable policy of *vaccination*. Deliberately a major scandal is exploded about a minor event—Watergate, the ITT case in 1973—in order to better hide and render more *acceptable* (according to Faye's definition) the true scandals: political assassinations, the coup d'état of September. You inoculate the public with a minor scandal; then when more serious things happen, the subject has already been deprived of most of its sensation value, its topical importance no longer has the aspect of novelty—the two fundamental criteria for big headlines in the newspapers.[7]

N.C.: Yes, that is in keeping with what I've just said about the liberal press since the end of the war. The government has great need now to restore its credibility, to make people forget history, and to rewrite it. The intelligentsia have to a remarkable degree undertaken this task. It is also necessary to establish the "lessons" that have to be drawn from the war, to ensure that these are conceived on the narrowest grounds, in terms of such socially neutral categories as "stupidity" or "error" or "ignorance" or perhaps "cost."

Why? Because soon it will be necessary to justify other confrontations, perhaps other U.S. interventions in the world, other Vietnams.

But this time, these will have to be successful interventions, which don't slip out of control. Chile, for example. It is even possible for the press to criticize successful interventions—the Dominican Republic, Chile, etc.—as long as these criticisms don't exceed "civilized limits," that is to say, as long as they don't serve to arouse popular movements capable of hindering these enterprises, and are not accompanied by any rational analysis of the motives of U.S. imperialism, something which is complete anathema, intolerable to liberal ideology.

How is the liberal press proceeding with regard to Vietnam, that sector which supported the "doves"? By stressing the "stupidity" of the U.S. intervention; that's a politically neutral term. It would have been sufficient to find an "intelligent" policy. The war was thus a tragic error in which good intentions were transmuted into bad policies, because of a generation of incompetent and arrogant officials. The war's savagery is also denounced; but that too is used as a neutral category . . . Presumably the goals were legitimate—it would have been all right to do the same thing, but more humanely . . .

The "responsible" doves were opposed to the war—on a pragmatic basis. Now it is necessary to reconstruct the system of beliefs according to which the United States is the benefactor of humanity, historically committed to freedom, self-determination, and human rights. With regard to this doctrine, the "responsible" doves share the same presuppositions as the hawks: they do not question the right of the United States to intervene in other countries. Their criticism is actually very convenient for the state, which is quite willing to be chided for its errors, as long as the fundamental right of forceful intervention is not brought into question.

Take a look at this editorial in the *New York Times,* offering a retrospective analysis of the Vietnam war as it came to an end. The editors feel that it is too early to draw conclusions about the war:

> Clio, the goddess of history, is cool and slow and elusive in her ways. . . . Only later, much later, can history begin to make an assessment of the mixture of good and evil, of wisdom and folly, of ideals and illusions in the long Vietnam story. . . . There are those Americans who believe that the war to preserve a non-Communist, independent South Vietnam could have been waged differently. There are other Americans who believe that a viable, non-Communist South Vietnam was always a myth. . . . A decade of fierce polemics has failed to resolve this ongoing quarrel.

You see, they don't even mention the logical possibility of a third position: namely, that the United States did not have the right, either the legal or the moral right, to intervene by force in the internal affairs of Vietnam. We leave to history the task of judging the debate between the hawks and the respectable doves, but the third position, opposed to the other two, is excluded from discussion. The sphere of Clio does not extend to such absurd ideas as the belief that the United States has no unique right to intervene with force in the internal affairs of others, whether such intervention is successful or not. The *Times* published many letters responding to its editorial, but no letter questioning the alternatives presented. I know for certain that at least one such letter was sent to them* . . . quite possibly many others.

April 8, 1975

To the Editor
New York Times
229 West 43d St.
New York, N.Y. 10036

Dear Sir:

An editorial in the *Times,* April 5, observes that "a decade of fierce polemics has failed to resolve this ongoing quarrel" between two contending views: that "the war to preserve a non-Communist, independent South Vietnam could have been waged differently," and that "a viable, non-Communist South Vietnam was always a myth." There has also been a third position: That apart from its prospects for success, the United States has neither the authority nor competence to intervene in the internal affairs of Vietnam. This was the position of much of the authentic peace movement, that is, those who opposed the war because it was wrong, not merely because it was unsuccessful. It is regrettable that this position is not even a contender in the debate, as the *Times* sees it.

On a facing page, Donald Kirk observes that "since the term 'bloodbath' first came into vogue in the Indochinese conflict, no one seems to have applied it to the war itself— only to the possible consequences of ending the war." He is quite wrong. Many Americans involved in the authentic peace movement have insisted for years on the elementary point that he believes has been noticed by "no one," and it is a commonplace in literature on the war. To mention just one example, we have written a small book on the subject (*Counterrevolutionary Violence: Bloodbaths in Fact and*

---

*Translator's note: Noam Chomsky has made available the letter he and Professor Edward S. Herman sent to the *New York Times.* I would like to take the opportunity to make this letter public at this late date, both for its intrinsic interest and to illustrate the limits imposed on public discussion in our leading newspaper.

Propaganda, 1973), though in this case the corporation (Warner Brothers) that owned the publisher refused to permit distribution after publication. But quite apart from this, the observation has been made repeatedly in discussion and literature on the war, by just that segment of opinion that the *Times* editorial excludes from the debate.

Sincerely yours,

Noam Chomsky
Professor, MIT

Edward S. Herman
Professor, University
of Pennsylvania

NC/ESH: lt

Note that as the *Times* sets the spectrum of debate, the position of much of the peace movement is simply excluded from consideration. Not that it is wrong, but rather unthinkable, inexpressible. As the *Times* sets the ground rules, the basic premises of the state propaganda system are presupposed by all participants in the debate: the American goal was to preserve an "independent" South Vietnam—perfect nonsense, as is easy to demonstrate—and the only question that arises is whether this worthy goal was within our grasp or not. Even the more audacious propaganda systems rarely go so far as to put forth state doctrine as unquestionable dogma, so that criticism of it need not even be rejected, but may simply be ignored.

Here we have a marvelous illustration of the functioning of propaganda in a democracy. A totalitarian state simply enunciates official doctrine—clearly, explicitly. Internally, one can think what one likes, but one can only express opposition at one's peril. In a democratic system of propaganda no one is punished (in theory) for objecting to official dogma. In fact, dissidence is encouraged. What this system attempts to do is to fix the limits of possible thought: supporters of official doctrine at one end, and the critics—vigorous, courageous, and much admired for their independence of judgment—at the other. The hawks and the doves. But we discover that all share certain tacit assumptions, and that it is these assumptions that are really crucial. No doubt a propaganda system is more effective when its doctrines are insinuated rather than asserted, when it sets the bounds for possible thought rather than simply imposing a clear and easily identifiable doctrine that one must parrot—or suffer the consequences. The more vigorous the debate, the more effectively the basic doctrines of the propaganda system, tacitly assumed on all sides, are instilled. Hence the elaborate pretense that the press is a critical dissenting force—maybe even too critical for the health of democracy—when in fact it is almost entirely subservient to the basic principles of the ideological system: in this case, the principle of the right of intervention, the unique right of the United States to serve as global judge and executioner. It is quite a marvelous system of indoctrination.

Here is still another example along the same lines. Look at this quotation from the Washington *Post,* a paper that is often regarded as the most consistent critic of the war among the national media. This is from an editorial of April 30, 1975, entitled "Deliverance":

> For if much of the actual conduct of Vietnam policy over the years was wrong and misguided—even tragic—it cannot be denied that some part of the purpose of that policy was right and defensible. Specifically, it was right to hope that the people of South Vietnam would be able to decide on their own form of government and social order. The American public is entitled, indeed obligated, to explore how good impulses came to be transmuted into bad policy, but we cannot afford to cast out all remembrance of that earlier impulse.

What were the "good impulses"? When precisely did the United States try to help the South Vietnamese choose their own form of government and social order? As soon as such questions are posed, the absurdity becomes evident. From the moment that the American-backed French effort to destroy the major nationalist movement in Vietnam collapsed, the United

States was consciously and knowingly opposed to the organized political forces within South Vietnam, and resorted to increasing violence when these political forces could not be crushed. But these facts, easily documented, must be suppressed. The liberal press cannot question the basic doctrine of the state religion, that the United States is benevolent, even though often misguided in its innocence, that it labors to permit free choice, even though at times some mistakes are committed in the exuberance of its programs of international goodwill. We must believe that we "Americans" are always good, though, to be sure, fallible:

> For the fundamental "lesson" of Vietnam surely is not that we as a people are intrinsically bad, but rather that we are capable of error—and on a gigantic scale. . . .

Note the rhetoric: "we as a people" are not intrinsically bad, even if we are capable of error. Was it "we as a people" who decided to conduct the war in Vietnam? Or was it something that had rather more to do with our political leaders and the social institutions they serve? To pose such a question is of course illegitimate, according to the dogmas of the state religion, because that raises the question of the institutional sources of power, and such questions are only considered by irrational extremists who must be excluded from debate (we can raise such questions with regard to other societies, of course, but not the United States).

It is not out of pessimism that I believe in the effectiveness of such techniques of legitimation of U.S. interventions, as a basis for future actions. One must not forget that while the U.S. government suffered a setback in Vietnam, it succeeded only too well in Indonesia, in Chile, in Brazil, and in many other places during the same period.

The resources of imperialist ideology are quite vast. It tolerates—indeed, encourages—a variety of forms of opposition, such as those I have just illustrated. It is permissible to criticize the lapses of the intellectuals and of government advisers, and even to accuse them of an abstract desire for "domination," again a socially neutral category, not linked in any way to concrete social and economic structures. But to relate that abstract "desire for domination" to the employment of force by the United States government in order to preserve a certain system of world order, specifically, to ensure that the countries of the world remain open insofar as possible to exploitation by U.S.-based corporations—that is extremely impolite, that is to argue in an unacceptable way.

In the same way, the respectable members of the academic world must ignore the substantial documentation concerning the principles that guide U.S. foreign policy, and its concern to create a global economic order that conforms to the needs of the U.S. economy and its masters. I'm referring, for example, to the crucial documentation contained in the *Pentagon Papers,* covering the late 1940s and early 1950s, when the basic policies were clearly set, or the documents on global planning for the postwar period produced in the early 1940s by the War-Peace Studies groups of the Council on Foreign Relations, to mention only two significant examples. Quite generally, the question of the influence of corporations on foreign policy, or the economic factors in policy formation, are reserved for the barest mention in a footnote in respectable studies of the formation of policy, a fact that has been occasionally studied, and is easily documented when studied.

M.R.: To reveal the profits of "philanthrophy," that is hardly in good taste.

In fact, all that you have been saying suggests to me a curious convergence, in the form of a provisional conclusion, that goes back to the initial question: What can the links be between a theory of ideology and the concepts of your linguistic theory, generative grammar?

The imperialist ideology, you say, can readily tolerate a quite large number of contradictions, infractions, and criticisms—all these remain acceptable, *except one:* to reveal the economic motives. You have a situation of the same kind in generative poetics. I am thinking of the analysis which Halle and Keyser[8] proposed for English iambic pentameter.

The verse has a structure of alternating strong and weak stresses:

$$WS, \ WS, \ WS, \ WS, \ WS,$$
(where W = weak and S = strong)

But if one studies the corpus of English poetry, one finds an enormous number of contradictions to the meter, of "infractions" of the dominant schema, and these verses are not only acceptable but often even the most beautiful. *One thing only is forbidden:* to make a weak position in the meter (in the abstract verse schema) correspond to a stressed vowel surrounded by two unstressed vowels. (Halle and Keyser's concept of "maximum stress.")

The observation of this kind of forbidden statement in the media permits the hope that the theory of ideology can reveal the objective laws which underlie political discourse; but for the time being all that is only a metaphor.

CHAPTER 2

Linguistics and the Human Sciences

M.R.:   There has been a good deal of question during these last years about "interdisciplinary studies," about establishing closer links between neighboring disciplines. What do you think of the way in which the relationship between linguistics and psychology has been presented?

N.C.:   In my opinion one should not speak of a "relationship" between linguistics and psychology, because linguistics is *part of* psychology; I cannot conceive of it in any other way.

In general, the following distinction is often made: linguistics is the study of language, and psychology the study of the acquisition or utilization of language. This distinction does not seem to me to make much sense. No discipline can concern itself in a productive way with the acquisition or utilization of a form of knowledge, without being concerned with the *nature* of that system of knowledge.

If psychology were to limit itself to the study of models of learning or perception or speech while excluding from its field of investigation the system itself that is thus acquired or utilized, it would condemn itself to sterility. That kind of delimitation of psychology would be quite pointless.

At this point, linguistics understood as the study of the system of language seems to fill a conceptual gap in the manner in which psychology is often conceived. In effect, it makes possible a psychology of language which is concerned at the same time with the system that is acquired *and* the ways in which it is acquired and used. This direction offers great hopes. At the same time, a linguistics which concerns itself solely with the system that is acquired and not with the manner in which it is acquired or the ways in which it is put to use confines itself within too narrow limits, and omits the consideration of issues that may have great importance for its narrower goals, which are of great interest in themselves.

Psychology of language, properly understood, is a discipline which embraces the study of the acquired system (the grammar), of the methods of acquisition (linked to universal grammar), and models of perception and production, and which also studies the physical bases for all of this. This study forms a coherent whole. Results obtained in the study of one of the parts may contribute to the understanding of the others. Take the work of Jerry Fodor in psycholinguistics . . .

Mr.R.:   If my memory is correct, he conducts experiments that consist of inserting noises or "clicks" at precise places on a magnetic tape on which sentences have been recorded, and then asking the subjects of the experiment the exact location in the sentence where they have perceived, or heard, these "clicks."

N.C.:   Yes. And in principle this work might help to resolve controversial problems of linguistic structure. Take the case of the grammatical transformation called "raising." This is an operation which has been postulated for such constructions as *John expected Bill to leave.* This operation takes the subject of the embedded clause *Bill leaves* and "raises" it to the position of object of the main verb (*John expected that—Bill leaves* thus becomes *John expected—Bill—to leave*). Let us take another sentence, which superficially resembles *John expected Bill to leave: John persuaded Bill to leave.* The click experiments might in principle tell us whether these sentences have the same structure. Suppose that in the recording of the two sentences, a click is inserted over the word *Bill.* If the click is perceived before *Bill* in the case of *expected* and after *Bill* in the case of *persuaded,* and if furthermore it is established that the perceptual displacement of the clicks depends on the surface syntactic structure, then one could conclude that the respective structures are:

> *(John expected (Bill to leave))*
>
> and   *(John (persuaded Bill) (to leave)).*

If, on the other hand, the relevant experiments show that the perceived displacement of the clicks is the same in both cases, that is to say, if the click placed over *Bill* is displaced perceptually to the right (i.e., after *Bill*), that would indicate that "raising" has taken place, and that the subject of the embedded phrase has become the object of *expect.*

Such results might contribute to resolving the problem of whether "raising" takes place in these structures. To be sure, it is too early to hope for definitive answers from such experiments. But the logic of the situation is sufficiently clear. It is possible that significant relationships between perception and sentence structure will be experimentally demonstrated. In fact, anyone who is interested in the structure of language will hope for the development of such experimental techniques, because then one would have means for empirically testing theories of language structure through the study of models of perception, and vice versa.

Furthermore, we might expect that any progress made in the psychology of language will furnish suggestive models for other aspects of cognitive psychology (such as visual perception, formation of theories about the external world, whether those of common sense or of scientific research, etc.), which might be studied profitably in a similar manner: that is, by determining the basic properties of the acquired cognitive systems *and* by investigating the processes of acquisition and use of these systems.

Cognitive psychology would thus study each cognitive system as a particular "mental organ," having its own structure, and subsequently investigating their modes of interaction. For such modes of interaction exist: when we see something, we are in general capable of speaking about it, and command of appropriate terminology may play some role in sharpening visual perception. There is the possibility for a kind of "translation" between visual representation and spoken language. The same is true for other systems. Linguistics is one part of cognitive psychology: a part that is relatively easy to isolate. Language is a system (very rich, to be sure), but easy to isolate, among the various mental faculties.

M.R.:   It is clear that the psychology you founded, by filling the conceptual "gap" that inheres in the sciences of behavior with the theory of generative grammar, is very different from that experimental psychology which has been presented to us for a long time now, be it by Skinner or by Piaget. We are far removed from intelligence quotients and the absolute faith in tests.

N.C.:   Many people tend to think of psychology in terms of its tests and experimental methods. But one should not define a discipline by its procedures. It should be defined, in the first place, by the object of its investigation. Experimental or analytic procedures must be devised in order to shed light on this object. Behaviorist psychology, for example, excels in its experimental techniques, but it has not properly defined its object of inquiry, in my opinion. Thus it has excellent tools, very good tools . . . but nothing very much to study with them.

M.R.:   It was with this critique of behaviorism that you began your philosophic work. In your review article on Skinner, which appeared in *Language* in 1959, you rejected the scientific pretensions of the experimental methods which proceed by stimulus-response reinforcement and "operant conditioning," used to study animal behavior. For example, Skinner considers it of interest to ask X number of subjects what a painting of the Flemish School evokes for them. The elicited response that would be judged "good" by Skinner is: "For me it evokes Holland." However, you have pointed out that one could reply: "I feel the painting is hung too low," or "In my opinion the painting clashes with the flowered wallpaper." These experiments, you wrote, are as simple as they are empty.

N.C.: I must add that quite similar critiques were made by Wolfgang Köhler and by other Gestalt psychologists many years before, but with little effect. And we must not forget that, as I've just said, many of the experiments that have been developed show considerable ingenuity and elegance. Certainly one must preserve the experimental sophistication of behaviorist psychology, but in order to employ it rationally. The same thing is true in physics: perhaps there are more sophisticated experimental techniques than those devised by physicists to answer interesting questions, but which have no relevance to questions of scientific interest. It would then be senseless to define physics in terms of this technology of experimentation. In itself this technology has no interest, apart from its possible relevance to significant questions.

In the same way, psychological experiments have no interest, unless they can be put to use to sharpen our understanding of significant theories that can be developed concerning some significant object of study.

M.R.: Are there many psychologists who are working in the direction you have just defined, who are interested at the same time in the linguistic system and in the principles of its acquisition?

N.C.: Quite a few in this country. In France you have Jacques Mehler, for one. It is becoming an important field, and I hope to remain in close contact with it.

M.R.: But does experimental psycholinguistics always serve solely to verify linguists' hypotheses, or do you consider it a field with its own goals?

N.C.: As I mentioned before, there is in principle an interplay between the study of the structure of language (that part of psychology called "linguistics") and experimental psycholinguistics, which is largely concerned with models of perception and production. I am personally interested in the possibility of testing linguistic hypotheses. Certain questions cannot be resolved by sole reliance on the customary methods of linguistics. For example: the study of temporal processes, constraints on memory, the interactions between cognitive systems. Furthermore, the abstract study of grammar, and the kinds of data utilized by linguists, are simply insufficient to resolve certain questions concerning language. Linguistics can hope to characterize the class of possible grammars, that is, establish the abstract properties which every language must satisfy. Similarly, study of a particular language can at best specify abstract properties of its grammar. It is something like the study of algebra: every abstract algebra can be realized by many different real systems. The theory of groups can be realized by the number system, or by the rotation of objects. In a similar way the formal systems of the linguists can correspond to different real systems . . .

M.R.: Just as in metrics, according to Morris Halle, the same abstract representation—XXXXXX, for example—can correspond to six vowels for the poet, to six roses for the gardener, or to six steps for the dancer . . .

N.C.: And if the linguist is interested in the real nature of human beings—which is what I suppose—then he will seek to discover the system that is really utilized. The data of linguistics are not rich enough to answer these fascinating questions beyond a certain point. Therefore, the linguist must hope for further insight from the study of process models and neurological structures.

M.R.: The linguistic model is a model of what is termed *competence.* You have just mentioned process models or models of *performance.* This opposition, *competence-performance,* was first clearly stated around 1964–5. You defined linguistic *competence* as that knowledge internalized by a speaker of a language, which, once learned and possessed, unconsciously permits him to understand and produce an infinite number of new sentences. *Generative grammar* is the explicit theory proposed to account for that competence. In performance, other cognitive systems, aside from competence (memory, etc.), intervene.

In *Language and Mind* you indicate that the other branches of psychology—dealing with vision, memory, and so on—must, in order to become scientific, define an equivalent concept of competence. Now it is evident that most psychologists oppose just that concept.

N.C.: In my opinion, many psychologists have a curious definition of their discipline. A definition that is destructive, suicidal. A dead end. They want to confine themselves solely to the study of performance—behavior—yet, as I've said, it makes no sense to construct a discipline that studies the manner in which a system is acquired or utilized, but refuses to consider the nature of this system.

In my opinion, in order to do good psychology one must start by identifying a cognitive domain—vision, for example—that is to say, a domain which can be considered as a system, or a mental organ, that is more or less integrated. Once that system is identified, one can try to determine its nature, to investigate theories concerning its structure. To the extent that such a theory can be formulated, it is possible to ask on what basis the system is acquired, what are the analogues in it to universal grammar, its biologically given principles. Similarly, study of performance presupposes an understanding of the nature of the cognitive system that is put to use. Given some level of theoretical understanding of some cognitive system, we may hope to study in a productive way how the cognitive system is used, and how it enters into interaction with other cognitive systems. Something like that should be the paradigm for psychology, I think. Of course, this is an oversimplification. One cannot legislate the "order of discovery." But this paradigm seems to me basically correct.

M.R.: That is the approach which you have followed in linguistics. You have identified the system: the *competence*—

and you have proposed a theory, that of *generative grammar*. Universal grammar is the set of hypotheses that bear on the acquisition of the system and so on. But such is not the customary path of psychology.

N.C.:   No, because until fairly recently psychologists have tried to leap over the initial stages; and going directly to the subsequent stages, they have been unable to accomplish as much as they could. Because you cannot study the acquisition or use of language in an intelligent manner without having some idea about this language which is acquired or utilized. If all you know of language is that it consists of words, or if you have a theory of the Saussurean type that tells you: "Here is a sequence of signs, each having a sound and a meaning," that limits very greatly the type of process model you can investigate. You must work with performance models, which produce word-by-word sequences, with no higher structure. You can only work with acquisition models, which acquire a system of concepts and sounds, and with the relations between these systems. That would be a primitive psychology, limited by the conception of language that was the point of departure. The same holds quite generally.

Psychologists often say that they don't presuppose a model of competence, that is to say, a theory of language. But that is not true; they could not do anything without having a conception of the nature of language. Every psychologist presupposes at least that language is a system of words: that is a model of competence. A very bad model of competence, but a model just the same. If they want to do better psychology, they must choose a better model of competence.

Why are many psychologists reluctant to consider richer and more abstract models of competence? Many linguists too, for the matter. In my opinion, because they are still under the influence of empiricist doctrines that are restricted in principle to quite elementary models of competence. These doctrines maintain that all learning, including language acquisition, proceeds by the accumulation of specific items, by the development

of associations, by generalization along certain stimulus dimen-
sions, by abstracting certain properties from a complex of properties. If this is the case, the models of competence are so trivial
that it is possible to ignore them.

M.R.: When looked at this way, the Saussurean system of
signs, conceived as a *store* slowly deposited in memory, corresponds very well, in effect, with the trivial empiricist model.

Do you know Gregory's experiments on vision? They prove
that vision is produced by an interaction between an innate
system and experience.

N.C.: Gregory is one of those who are trying to construct
a model of *competence* for vision. That is interesting work, and
it seems a logical way to treat these questions. Apparently, the
visual cortex of mammals is predetermined in part, with a
certain margin of indeterminacy. There exist, for example, cells
of the visual cortex which are designed to perceive lines at a
certain angle, and others at another angle; but the development
of these receptors, their *density*, in particular, or their precise
orientation within a predetermined range of potential orientation, all this depends on the visual environment, so it appears.

M.R.: Vision is thus a construction, like grammar?

N.C.: It seems that the general structure of the visual system is fixed, but the particular detailed realization remains
open. For example, it is supposedly virtually impossible to determine precise binocular coordination genetically. It seems
that visual experience is required to solve this engineering problem in a precise way, though binocular vision is genetically
determined.

In general, serious psychology will be concerned primarily
with domains in which human beings excel, where their capacities are exceptional. Language is one such case. There one is
sure to find rich structures to study. In the domain of visual
perception, for example, one of the most extraordinary abilities
is to identify faces. How can one, after having seen a face from
a certain angle, recognize it from another angle? That involves
a remarkable geometric transformation. And to distinguish two

faces! It would be no small task to design a device to match human performance in these respects.

It is possible that the theory of face perception resembles a generative grammar. Just as in language, if you suppose that there are base structures and transformed structures, then one might imagine a model which would generate the possible human faces, and the transformations which would tell you what each face would look like from all angles. To be sure, the formal theories would be very different from those of language ...

M.R.:   ... because we are passing from linear sequence to volume.

N.C.:   There has also been very interesting work recently on the perceptual system of infants. During the past few years experimental methods have been devised that permit one to work with very young infants, even just a few days old, or a few weeks, and to determine some aspects of their perceptual systems, which exist, evidently, prior to relevant experience. It has been reported, for example, that infants distinguish the phonetic categories P, T, and K, which acoustically form a continuum: there is no line of demarcation between these categories, and no physical necessity to divide the acoustic continuum just this way. But perceptually they do not form a continuum. Particular stimuli along this dimension will be perceived as P or T or K. It seems that infants already make this categorial distinction, which indicates that it must reflect part of the human perceptual system that is not learned, but is rather an innate capacity, perhaps specifically related to language, though this is debated.

There is other work, on surprise reflexes, for example: if you present a small circle to a baby, which becomes a large circle, the infant will be startled. But if you present a circle, the size of which diminishes, there is no startle response. Such results have been reported informally, but I'm not sure that they have already been published or how firm they are. If they are correct, they suggest that there exists a mechanism, in effect innate, to recognize an approaching object. At the time this reflex does not have any function: the baby cannot move away in any fashion. That reflex would be built into the human perceptual system, and to find a functional explanation for it one would perhaps have to go back millions of years, to arrive at some evolutionary explanation.

M.R.: Can they see when they are that young?

N.C.: Again until recently, it was not known to what extent infants could see. One did not have any means of establishing that. Apparently, there is fairly complex visual perception well before the child can move. In any case, very early. One can also perhaps study linguistic capacities—as well as deficiencies, aphasia, and so forth—by similar methods.

There has been quite a bit of interesting work on the neurology of language, for example, on lateralization or the functions of the two hemispheres of the brain. Language is normally a left-hemisphere function primarily, and current work aims to clarify the specific functions of the two hemispheres. For instance, Bever has reported some work suggesting that musical analysis is carried out by the left side of the brain, which is concerned with analytic processing, while the right side keeps a sort of sensory account. That would be interesting if correct. While the phenomenon of lateralization does not occur solely among humans, it is in them that it is most highly developed.

These different lines of research are mutually supportive. In the coming years they may constitute one of the most exciting parts of science.

M.R.: You do not mention sociology. However, sociolinguistics seem to have been widely accepted. This discipline seeks to look at the facts of language as realities produced by social classes. I'm thinking particularly of Labov's[1] work on non-standard English of the ghettos. In my opinion, that is also linguistics.

N.C.: The study of various dialects certainly falls squarely within linguistics. But I do not see in what way the study of ghetto dialects differs from study of the dialects of university-trained speakers, from a purely linguistic point of view. On the theoretical level that is much the same thing. In fact, there are some who claim at times that there are certain theories concerning the study of language in society. Perhaps so, but I have not as yet *seen* such theories, or any specific account of the principles involved. Very few theoretical proposals have been made about these questions, to my knowledge.

Certainly, it is true that no individual speaks a well-defined language. The notion of language itself is on a very high level of abstraction. In fact, each individual employs a number of linguistic systems in speaking. How can one describe such an amalgam? Linguists have generally, and quite properly, proceeded in terms of an idealization: Let us assume, they say, the notion of a homogeneous linguistic community. Even if they don't admit it, that is what they do. It is the sole means of proceeding rationally, so it seems to me. You study ideal systems, then afterwards you can ask yourself in what manner these ideal systems are represented and interact in real individuals. Perhaps sociolinguistics might come up with some sort of principle concerning the variety of such systems, though I know of no results of this sort. It has been suggested that the language system of an individual does not consist in the interaction of ideal systems, but in a single system with some margin of variation. If that is it, then it's not very interesting.

I agree with what you say: that is part of linguistics. A linguistics that takes the idealization of ordinary linguistics one step closer to the complexity of reality. Fine.

M.R.:   I think it is very important for Labov to show that the language of the ghetto has a grammar of its own, which is not defined as a collection of errors or infractions of standard English . . .

N.C.:   . . . But who could doubt that? No linguist could possibly doubt that.

M.R.:   All right, because linguists know that this is a linguistic principle. But Labov is primarily addressing teachers, pedagogues who do not recognize, in general, the legitimacy of the spoken language, and who, besides, have the ideological task of inculcating a feeling of inferiority in those who do not speak the standard dialect.

N.C.: He is doing something very useful on the level of educational practice, in attempting to combat the prejudices of the society at large—and that is very good. But on the linguistic level, this matter is evident and banal. Stone Age man spoke a language similar to ours, so far as we know. It is evident that the language of the ghettos is of the same order as that of the suburbs. The study of Black English, from a linguistic point of view, is on a par with the study of Korean or of American Indian languages, or of the difference between the English of Cambridge, England, and Cambridge, Massachusetts. That is very useful work. But what disturbs me are the theoretical pretensions. We have here good descriptive linguistics, but it takes no sophistication in linguistics to establish the socially relevant conclusion. The same ideological aim is attained, for example, by Theodore Rosengarten in his book, *All God's Dangers,* which is the autobiography of Nate Shaw. Rosengarten transcribed the narrative of an old black man, who was illiterate and who had preserved an astonishing memory of his entire life. He was a sort of natural storyteller, whose life, involved in historic social struggles, is fascinating. Rosengarten, transcribing the spoken narration of this old man, is saying much the same thing as what you attribute to Labov: this man is also a human being, in fact, a human being who was altogether remarkable.

Perhaps some confusion arises from one of my statements, which has provoked more controversy than I had foreseen: I spoke of the necessity to conceive of a homogeneous linguistic community . . .

M.R.: . . . As an idealization necessary for scientific work. Which, as you wrote, does not mean that reality is homogeneous; but such an idealization is necessary, in fact, automatic even, when one studies the language of the ghettos.

N.C.: Of course. And all dialects. In my opinion, this is the rational way to approach the study of dialect variations: we are still always speaking of idealized systems. Only such systems have interesting properties. Combinations of systems rarely have interesting properties. Let me take an example: as a small child, my friend Morris Halle spoke five languages. Taken together these five languages do not have interesting properties. Individually, they do. In the same way, if someone speaks a collection of dialects, you will only discover a great confusion if you do not separate the elements of which this ensemble is composed.

M.R.:   Nevertheless, it seems important to me to confront the progressive work of Labov with the position in psycholinguistics of someone like Bernstein,[2] who reinforces and justifies social discrimination.

N.C.:   The work of Bernstein may very well be reactionary in its implications, and perhaps hardly worth discussing as a specimen of the rational study of language. I had believed it should no longer be necessary to say that the spoken language of an urban ghetto is a real language. But perhaps that's not the case. Some educators, and others, seem to take seriously the hypothesis about the severe limitations of competence among the children of the "lower classes." But the existence of a discipline called "sociolinguistics" remains for me an obscure matter.

M.R.:   More generally, what does sociology mean to you today?

N.C.:   Again, a discipline is defined in terms of its object and its results. Sociology is the study of society. As to its results, it seems that there are few things one can say about that, at least at a fairly general level. One finds observations, intuitions, impressions, some valid generalizations perhaps. All very valuable, no doubt, but not at the level of explanatory principles. Literary criticism also has things to say, but it does not have explanatory principles. Of course ever since the ancient Greeks people have been trying to find general principles on which to base literary criticism, but, while I'm far from an authority in this field, I'm under the impression that no one has yet succeeded in establishing such principles. Very much as in other human sciences. That is not a criticism. It is a characterization, which seems to me to be correct. Sociolinguistics is, I suppose, a discipline that seeks to apply principles of sociology to the study of language; but I suspect that it can draw little from sociology, and I wonder whether it is likely to contribute much to it.

M.R.: In general one links a social class to a set of linguistic forms in a manner that is almost bi-unique.

N.C.: You can also collect butterflies and make many observations. If you like butterflies, that's fine; but such work must not be confounded with research, which is concerned to discover explanatory principles of some depth and fails if it does not do so.

M.R.: Certain sociologists accuse linguistics of participating in the legitimation of the dominant language, in particular because of the concept of "competence," which is often confused, more or less, with skill in handling the language. But above all, they reproach linguistics for its idealization, which removes it from social reality.

N.C.: Opposition to idealization is simply objection to rationality; it amounts to nothing more than an insistence that we shall not have meaningful intellectual work. Phenomena that are complicated enough to be worth studying generally involve the interaction of several systems. Therefore you *must* abstract some object of study, you must eliminate those factors which are not pertinent. At least if you want to conduct an investigation which is not trivial. In the natural sciences this isn't even discussed, it is self-evident. In the human sciences, people continue to question it. That is unfortunate. When you work within some idealization, perhaps you overlook something which is terribly important. That is a contingency of rational inquiry that has always been understood. One must not be too worried about it. One has to face this problem and try to deal with it, to accommodate oneself to it. It is inevitable.

There are no simple criteria that provide the correct idealization, unless it is the criterion of obtaining meaningful results.

If you obtain good results, then you have reason to believe that you are not far from a good idealization. If you obtain better results by changing your point of view, then you have improved your idealization. There is a constant interaction between the definition of the domain of research and the discovery of significant principles. To reject idealization is puerile. It is particularly strange to hear such criticism from the left. Marxist political economy furnishes a classic and familiar example, with its idealizations and its far-reaching abstractions.

M.R.:   Aren't sociologists seeking to preserve the methods they use at present, their interviews, surveys, statistics, and so on, which take the place of scientific practice?

N.C.:   Again, in itself this type of approach is neither good nor bad. The question is whether it leads to the discovery of principles that are significant. We are back to the difference between natural history and natural science. In natural history, whatever you do is fine. If you like to collect stones, you can classify them according to their color, their shape, and so forth. Everything is of equal value, because you are not looking for principles. You are amusing yourself, and nobody can object to that. But in the natural sciences, it is altogether different. There the search is for the discovery of intelligible structure and for explanatory principles. In the natural sciences, the facts have no interest in themselves, but only to the degree to which they have bearing on explanatory principles or on hidden structures that have some intellectual interest. I think this whole discussion comes down to a confusion between two senses of the word *interesting*. Certain things are interesting in themselves—for example: human action. When a novelist deals with human actions, that's interesting; the flight of a bird, a flower, that's interesting. In this sense, natural history and descriptive sociology are interesting, just like a novel. Both deal with interesting phenomena, and display these to our view, perhaps even yield insight into them, somehow.

But there is another meaning of the word *interesting*, in physics, for example. A phenomenon in itself does not have interest for a physicist. In fact, physicists are generally interested, at least in the modern period, in "exotic" phenomena, of virtually no interest in themselves, in the first sense of the word *interesting*. What happens under the conditions of a scientific experiment is of no importance in itself. Its interest lies in its relation to whatever theoretical principles are at stake. Natural science, as distinct from natural history, is not concerned with the phenomena in themselves, but with the principles and the explanations that they have some bearing on. There is no right or wrong in the choice of one of these definitions of the word *interesting* (or some other sense, relating to utility, for example). It is not wrong to be interested in human actions or right to be interested in particle accelerators. There are simply two entirely different things. The attraction of sociology should not be based on a confusion between the two senses of the word.

In the study of language, too, you find strange phenomena. In English you cannot say:

John seems to the men to like each other

meaning that John seems to each of the men to like the others. There is nothing wrong with the intended meaning; it is just that this sentence doesn't express it. In itself that does not have any interest; no one ever says it, and that's all there is to the matter. But it happens that the phenomenon has intellectual interest, because it is linked to significant principles of linguistic theory.

The problem in the human sciences is that practitioners can easily find themselves in the position of describing phenomena of little interest and having nothing interesting to say about their subject. That is the worst of all; presenting, say, statistical analyses on subjects that are without interest . . . To be sure, anthropology and sociology often achieve very interesting results. Take the work of my colleague Kenneth Hale, for example. He has been studying the "cultural wealth" of indigenous cultures and languages of Australia. These people can be characterized as among the most "primitive" in the world, at least from the point of view of technology. But they have developed intellectual systems which are extraordinarily complex, and language games which are incomparable . . .

M.R.: I remember reading his study of a game of antonyms, where each speaker must replace words by their opposites, according to certain rules . . .

N.C.: Yes, that is one example. What emerges from his work is very interesting, undoubtedly. These games could not have been invented simply to pass the time: they respond to fundamental intellectual needs. It has also been suggested that the proliferation of the extraordinarily complex and intricate systems of kinship may have no explanation in terms of social function . . .

M.R.: Thus he is opposed to the functionalism of Lévi-Strauss, which links the kinship system to exchange . . .

N.C.: Perhaps these kinship systems satisfy an intellectual need. They may be the kind of mathematics you can create if you don't have formal mathematics. The Greeks made up number theory, others make up kinship systems. Hale and others report informants who are exceptionally gifted in kinship systems, just as mathematicians can be gifted. These discoveries belong to anthropology, but naturally to psychology as well. They show how human beings create cultural richness under conditions of material privation. As far as these language games are concerned, children are said to have no difficulty at all in learning them. They seem to be linked to rites of puberty. All very strange and fascinating.

M.R.: These discoveries are "interesting" in both senses of the word.

It seems to me that the facts of language also offer these two ways of being interesting.

N.C.: Yes. Take a good traditional grammar: it presents those phenomena which have a "human" interest; for example, irregular verbs. Irregular verbs, that's amusing. But traditional grammar does not take interest in what some generative gram-

marians term the *specified subject condition,* * because the phenomena which are excluded by this condition have no "human
interest."

For example, the sentence I mentioned earlier, *John seems to
the men to like each other,* is excluded by the specified subject
condition. But I doubt that any traditional grammar, even the
most comprehensive one, would trouble to note that such sentences must be excluded. And that is quite legitimate, as far as
traditional grammars of English are concerned; these grammars appeal to the intelligence of the reader instead of seeking
explicitly to characterize this "intelligence." One can suppose
that the specified subject condition—or any other principle
which excludes this phrase—is simply an aspect of the intelligence of the speaker, an aspect of universal grammar; consequently, it does not require explicit instruction to the person
who reads a traditional grammar.

For the linguist, the opposite is true. The linguist is interested
in what the traditional grammars *don't say;* he is interested in
the principles—or at least that is what should interest him, in
my opinion.

M.R.: The typical reaction one encounters in the human
sciences, against idealization, thus seems linked to the fact that
people are not interested in what they have in common, but . . .

N.C.: . . . but in what differentiates them, yes. And in their
normal human lives, this is the right decision. The same thing
must be true of frogs. No doubt, they would not be interested

---

*This is a condition which forbids both the extraction of an element belonging to an
embedded phrase, and also its association with an element that is outside this phrase,
if the embedded phrase contains a "specified" subject—"specified" in a meaning of the
term which must be defined precisely. For example, in the sentence, *We expected John
to like each other,* the phrase *each other* cannot be associated with the antecedent
we, so that the sentence does not express the meaning, "Each of us expected that John
would like the other." The specified subject condition prevents this association, because
of the presence of the subject *John* in the embedded clause, *John to like each other.* The
same condition operates in the example given above: *John seems to the men to like each
other.* Here the subject of *like* is not phonetically present, but is "understood" to be
John. For a discussion of these questions, see Chomsky, *Reflections on Language* (New
York: Pantheon, 1975), chapter 3.

in what makes them frogs, but in what makes them different from one another: whether one jumps further, etc.; anything that makes a frog remarkable for other frogs. The frogs assume that it is perfectly natural to be a frog. They are not preoccupied by "frogness."

M.R.:   Among Americans, "frogs" is also used to designate the French . . .

N.C.:   I did not have that in mind.

CHAPTER 3

A Philosophy of Language

M.R.: Your linguistic discoveries have led you to take positions in philosophy of language and in what is called "philosophy of knowledge." In particular, in your last book (*Reflections on Language*), you were induced to determine the limits of what is *knowable in thought;* as a result, the reflections on language became transformed virtually into a philosophy of science . . .

N.C.: Of course, it is not the study of language that determines what is to count as a scientific approach; but in fact this study provides a useful model to which one can refer in the investigation of human knowledge.

In the case of language, one must explain how an individual, presented with quite limited data, develops an extremely rich system of knowledge. The child, placed in a linguistic community, is presented with a set of sentences that is limited and often imperfect, fragmented, and so on. In spite of this, in a very short time he succeeds in "constructing," in internalizing the grammar of his language, developing knowledge that is very complex, that cannot be derived by induction or abstraction from what is given in experience. We conclude that the internalized knowledge must be limited very narrowly by some biological property. Whenever we encounter a similar situation, where knowledge is constructed from limited and imperfect data in a manner that is uniform and homogeneous among all individuals, we can conclude that a set of initial constraints plays a significant role in determining the cognitive system which is constructed by the mind.

We find ourselves faced with what may seem a paradox, though it is in fact not a paradox at all: where rich and complex knowledge can be constructed in a uniform way, as in the case of knowledge of language, there must exist constraints, limitations imposed by biological endowment on the cognitive systems that can be developed by the mind. The scope of attainable knowledge is linked in a fundamental way with its limits.

M.R.:   If all kinds of grammatical rules were possible, then the acquisition of these rules would become impossible; if all combinations of phonemes were possible, there would no longer be language. The study of language shows, on the contrary, to what extent the sequential combinations of words, of phonemes, are limited, that these combinations form only a small subset of the set of imaginable combinations. Linguistics must render explicit the rules which limit these combinations. But on the basis of these limits one obtains an infinity of language forms . . .

N.C.:   If sharp limits on attainable knowledge did not exist, we could never have such extensive knowledge as that of language. For the simple reason that without these prior limitations, we could construct an enormous number of possible systems of knowledge, each compatible with what is given in experience. So the uniform attainment of some specific system of knowledge that extends far beyond experience would be impossible: we might adopt different cognitive systems, with no possibility of determining which of these systems is in fact the right one. If we have a considerable number of theories that are comparable in credibility, that is virtually the same as having no theory at all.

Let us suppose that we discover a domain of intelligence where human beings excel. If someone has developed a rich explanatory theory in spite of the limitations of available evidence, it is legitimate to ask what the general procedure is that has permitted this move from experience to knowledge—what is the system of constraints that has made possible such an intellectual leap.

The history of science might provide some relevant examples. At certain times, rich scientific theories have been constructed on the basis of limited data, theories that were intelligible to others, consisting of propositions linked in some manner to the nature of human intelligence. Given such cases, we might try to discover the initial constraints that characterize these theories. That leads us back to posing the question: What is the "universal grammar" for intelligible theories; what is the set of biologically given constraints?

Suppose we can answer this question—in principle that might be possible. Then, the constraints being given, we can inquire into the kinds of theories that can in principle be attained. This amounts to the same thing as when we ask, in the case of language: Given a theory of universal grammar, what types of languages are in principle possible?

Let us refer to the class of theories made available by the biological constraints as *accessible theories.* It may be that this class will not be homogeneous, that there will be degrees of accessibility, accessibility relative to other theories, etc. In other words, the theory of accessibility may be more or less structured. The "universal grammar" for theory construction is then a theory of the structure of accessible theories. If this "universal grammar" is part of the biological endowment of a person, then given appropriate evidence, the person will, in some cases at least, have certain accessible theories available. Admittedly, I'm simplifying greatly.

Consider then the class of *true* theories. We can imagine that such a class exists, expressed, let us say, in some notation available to us. Then we can ask: What is the *intersection* of the class of accessible theories and the class of true theories, that is to say, which theories belong at the same time to the class of accessible theories and to the class of true theories? (Or we can raise more complex questions about degree of accessibility and relative accessibility.) Where such an intersection exists, a human being can attain real knowledge. And conversely, he cannot attain real knowledge beyond that intersection.

Of course, this is on the assumption that the human mind is part of nature, that it is a biological system like others, perhaps more intricate and complex than others that we know about but a biological system nevertheless, with its potential scope and its intrinsic limits determined by the very factors that provide its scope. Human reason, on this view, is not the universal instrument that Descartes took it to be but rather a specific biological system.

M.R.:   We come back again to the idea according to which scientific activity is not possible except within the biological limits of the human being . . .

N.C.:   But notice that there is no particular biological reason why such an intersection should exist. The capacity to invent nuclear physics provides an organism with no selectional advantage, and was not a factor in human evolution, it is reasonable to assume. The ability to solve algebra problems is not a factor in differential reproduction. There is, to my knowledge, no credible version of the view that these special capacities are somehow continuous with practical abilities, toolmaking and the like—which is not to deny, of course, that these special capacities developed for unknown reasons as a concomitant of evolution of the brain that may have been subject to selectional pressures.

In a sense, the existence of an intersection of the class of accessible theories and the class of true theories is a kind of biological miracle. It seems that this miracle took place at least in one domain, namely, physics, and the natural sciences that one might think of loosely as a kind of "extension" of physics: chemistry, biochemistry, molecular biology. In these domains, progress has been extremely rapid on the basis of limited data, and in a manner intelligible to others. Perhaps we are confronted here with a unique episode in human history: there is nothing to lead one to believe that we are a universal organism. Rather, we are subject to biological limitations with respect to the theories we can devise and comprehend, and we are fortunate to have these limitations, for otherwise we could not construct rich systems of knowledge and understanding at all. But these limitations may well exclude domains about which we would like very much to know something. That's too bad. Perhaps there is another organism with a differently organized intelligence that would be capable of what we are not. This is, as a first approximation, a reasonable one in my opinion, a way to think about the question of acquisition of conscious knowledge.

Going a step further, it is not unimaginable that a particular organism might come to examine its *own* system of acquiring knowledge; it might thus be able to determine the class of intelligible theories which it can attain. I don't see any contradiction in that. A theory which is found to be unintelligible, an "inaccessible theory" in the sense just given, does not thereby become intelligible or accessible.

It would simply be identified. And if in some domain of thought the accessible theories turn out to be remote from the true theories, that's too bad. Then human beings can, at best, develop a kind of intellectual technology, which for inexplicable reasons predicts certain things in these domains. But they won't truly *understand* why the technology is working. They will not possess an intelligible theory in the sense that an interesting science is intelligible. Their theories, though perhaps effective, will be intellectually unsatisfying.

Looking at the history of human intellectual endeavor from this point of view, we find curious things, surprising things. In mathematics certain areas seem to correspond to exceptional human aptitudes: number theory, spatial intuition. Pursuit of these intuitions determined the main line of progress in mathematics, until the end of the nineteenth century, at least. Apparently our mind is capable of handling the abstract properties of number systems, abstract geometry, and the mathematics of the continuum. These are not the absolute limits, but it is probable that we are confined to certain branches of science and mathematics.

Presumably, all that I have just said would be rejected by a strict empiricist, or even regarded as senseless.

M.R.:   That is to say by someone who believes in the proposition according to which man proceeds by induction and generalization in the acquisition of knowledge, starting from "empty" or "blank" minds, without a priori biological limitations. Within that framework, knowledge is no more determined by the structure of the mind than is the form of a design by the wax tablet . . .

N.C.:   Yes. These empiricist hypotheses have very little plausibility, in my opinion; it does not seem possible to account for the development of commonsense understanding of the physical and social world, or science, in terms of processes of induction, generalization, abstraction, and so on. There is no such direct path from data that are given to intelligible theories.

The same is true in other domains, music, for example. After all, you can always imagine innumerable musical systems, most of which will seem to the human ear to be just noise. There too, biological factors determine the class of possible musical systems for human beings, though what exactly this class may be is an open and currently debated question.

In this case as well, no direct functional explanation seems available. Musical ability is not a factor in reproduction. Music does not improve material well-being, does not permit one to function better in society, etc. Quite simply, it responds to the human need for aesthetic expression. If we study human nature in a proper way, we may discover that certain musical systems correspond to that need, while others do not.

M.R.:   Among those fields in which the scientific approach has not made any progress in two thousand years you list the study of human behavior.

N.C.:   Behavior, yes, that is one such case. The basic questions have been posed since the beginning of historical memory:

the question of causation of behavior seems simple enough to pose, but virtually no theoretical progress has been made in answering it. One might formulate the basic question as follows: Consider a function of certain variables such that, given the values of the variables, the function will give us the behavior that results under the conditions specified by these values, or perhaps some distribution over possible behaviors. But no such function has been seriously proposed, even to a weak approximation, and the question has remained without issue. In fact, we don't know of any reasonable way to approach the problem. It is conceivable that this persistent failure is to be explained on the grounds that the true theory of behavior is beyond our cognitive reach. Therefore we can make no progress. It would be as if we tried to teach a monkey to appreciate Bach. A waste of time . . .

M.R.: Then the question of behavior would be different from the question of syntax: that too had never been posed before the development of generative grammar.

N.C.: But in this case, once the question is posed, everyone comes up with answers that are similar or comparable. When certain questions are posed, sometimes the answer is impossible to imagine, sometimes answers begin to appear quite widely. And when an answer is proposed, those who have an adequate understanding of the question will also regard the answer as intelligible. It is often the case that a question cannot yet properly be posed, or posed with the requisite degree of sophistication; but then it can sometimes be posed properly, and still seem to lie beyond our intellectual grasp.

Another analogue to the case of language, perhaps, is our comprehension of the social structures in which we live. We have all sorts of tacit and complex knowledge concerning our relations to other people. Perhaps we have a sort of "universal grammar" of possible forms of social interaction, and it is this system which helps us to organize intuitively our imperfect perceptions of social reality, though it does not follow necessarily that we are capable of developing conscious theories in

this domain through the exercise of our "science-forming faculties." If we succeed in finding our place within our society, that
is perhaps because these societies have a structure that we are
prepared to seek out. With a little imagination we could devise
an artificial society in which no one could ever find his place . . .

M.R.:   Then you can compare the failure of artificial languages with the failure of utopian societies?

N.C.:   Perhaps. One cannot learn an artificial language constructed to violate universal grammar as readily as one learns
a natural language, simply by being immersed in it. At most,
one might conceive of such a language as a game, a puzzle . . .
In the same way we can imagine a society in which no one could
survive as a social being because it does not correspond to
biologically determined perceptions and human social needs.
For historical reasons, existing societies might have such properties, leading to various forms of pathology.

Any serious social science or theory of social change must be
founded on some concept of human nature. A theorist of classical liberalism such as Adam Smith begins by affirming that
human nature is defined by a propensity to truck and barter, to
exchange goods: that assumption accords very well with the
social order he defends. If you accept that premise (which is
hardly credible), it turns out that human nature conforms to an
idealized early capitalist society, without monopoly, without
state intervention, and without social control of production.

If, on the contrary, you believe with Marx or the French and
German Romantics that only social cooperation permits the
full development of human powers, you will then have a very
different picture of a desirable society. There is always some
conception of human nature, implicit or explicit, underlying a
doctrine of social order or social change.

M.R.:   To what degree can your discoveries about language
and your definitions of fields of knowledge lead to the emergence of new philosophic questions? To which philosophy do
you feel closest?

N.C.:   In relation to the questions we have just been discussing, the philosopher to whom I feel closest and whom I'm almost paraphrasing is Charles Sanders Peirce. He proposed an interesting outline, very far from complete, of what he called "abduction" ...

M.R.: Abduction is, I believe, a form of inference which does not depend solely on a priori principles (like deduction), nor solely on experimental observation (like induction). But that aspect of Peirce is very little known in France.

N.C.: Or here in the United States either. Peirce argued that to account for the growth of knowledge, one must assume that "man's mind has a natural adaptation to imagining correct theories of some kinds," some principle of "abduction" which "puts a limit on admissible hypothesis," a kind of "instinct," developed in the course of evolution. Peirce's ideas on abduction were rather vague, and his suggestion that biologically given structure plays a basic role in the selection of scientific hypotheses seems to have had very little influence. To my knowledge, almost no one has tried to develop these ideas further, although similar notions have been developed independently on various occasions. Peirce has had an enormous influence, but not for this particular reason.

M.R.: More in semiology ...

N.C.: Yes, in that general area. His ideas on abduction developed Kantian ideas to which recent Anglo-American philosophy has not been very receptive. As far as I know, his approach in epistemology has never been followed up, even though there has been much criticism of inductivist approaches —Popper, for example.

Russell, for his part, was much preoccupied in his later work (*Human Knowledge*) with the inadequacy of the empiricist approach to the acquisition of knowledge. But this book has generally been ignored. He proposed various principles of *non-demonstrative inference* with the aim of accounting for the knowledge which in reality we possess.

M.R.: Non-demonstrative inference differs from the deductions of mathematical logic to the degree where, in spite of the truth of the premises and the rigorous character of the reasoning, the truth of the conclusions is not guaranteed; they are only rendered *probable.* Is that it?

N.C.:   In substance, yes: one might say that his approach here was Kantian to a certain degree, but with fundamental differences. In some way, Russell remained an empiricist. His principles of non-demonstrative inference are *added* one by one to the fundamental principle of induction, and do not offer a radical change in perspective. But the problem is not quantitative, it is qualitative. The principles of non-demonstrative inference do not fulfill the need. I believe a radically different approach is necessary, which takes a starting point that is quite remote from empiricist presuppositions. This is true not only for scientific knowledge, where it is generally accepted today, but also for what we can call the constructions of "common-sense understanding," that is, for our ordinary notions concerning the nature of the physical and social world, our intuitive comprehension of human actions, their ends, their reasons, and their causes, etc.

These are very important issues, which would demand much more analysis than I can give here. But to return to your question, a great deal of the work of contemporary philosophers on language and the nature of scientific research has been very stimulating for me. My own work, from the very beginning, was greatly influenced by developments in philosophy (as the published acknowledgments of indebtedness indicate; particularly, to Nelson Goodman and W. V. Quine). And that continues to be true. To mention only a few examples, the work of John Austin on speech acts proved very fruitful, as well as that of Paul Grice on the logic of conversation. At present very interesting work is being pursued on the theory of meaning along various lines. One can cite the contributions of Saul Kripke, Hilary Putnam, Jerrold Katz, Michael Dummett, Julius Moravcsik, Donald Davidson, and many others. Certain of the work on model-theoretic semantics—the study of "truth in possible worlds"—seems promising. In particular, I would mention the work of Jaakko Hintikka and his colleagues, which deals with questions that are central to quite a range of topics in syntax and semantics of natural languages, particularly with regard to quantification. Such work has also been extended to pragmatics, that is to the study of the manner in which language is used to accomplish certain human ends; for example, the work of the Israeli philosopher Asa Kasher. As these few brief references indicate, this work is being done on an international scale and is not just Anglo-American.

I should also mention work on history and philosophy of science, which has begun to furnish a richer and more exact understanding of the manner in which ideas develop and take root in the natural sciences. This work—for example, that of Thomas Kuhn or Imre Lakatós—has gone well beyond the often artificial models of verification and falsification, which were prevalent for a long time and which exercised a dubious influence on the "soft sciences," as the latter did not rest on the foundations of a healthy intellectual tradition that could guide their development. It is useful, in my opinion, for people working in these fields to become familiar with ways in which the natural sciences have been able to progress; in particular, to recognize how, at critical moments of their development, they have been guided by radical idealization, a concern for depth of insight and explanatory power rather than by a concern to accommodate "all the facts"—a notion that approaches meaninglessness—even at times disregarding apparent counterexamples in the hope (which at times has proven justified only after many years or even centuries) that subsequent insights would explain them. These are useful lessons that have been obscured in much of the discussion about epistemology and the philosophy of science.

M.R.: What do you think of European philosophers, of the French in particular?

N.C.: Outside of Anglo-American philosophy, I do not know enough about contemporary philosophers to discuss them at all seriously.

M.R.:   Have you ever met any French Marxist philosophers?

N.C.:   Rarely. Here some distinctions are necessary. Contemporary Marxist philosophy has been linked in large part to Leninist doctrine, at least until recently. European Marxism after World War I developed unfortunate tendencies, in my opinion: the tendencies associated with Bolshevism, which has always seemed to me an authoritarian and reactionary current. The latter became dominant within the European Marxist tradition after the Russian Revolution. But much more to my taste, at least, are quite different tendencies, for example, that range of opinion that extends roughly from Rosa Luxemburg and the Dutch Marxist Anton Pannekoek and Paul Mattick to the anarcho-syndicalist Rudolf Rocker and others.

These thinkers have not contributed to philosophy in the sense of our discussion; but they have much to say about society, about social change, and the fundamental problems of human life. Though not about problems of the sort that we have been discussing, for example.

Marxism itself has become too often a sort of church, a theology.

Of course, I'm generalizing far too much. Work of value has been done by those who consider themselves Marxists. But up to a certain point this criticism is justified, I'm afraid. In any case, I do not believe that Marxist philosophy, of whatever tendency, has made a substantial contribution to the kind of questions we have been discussing.

For the rest, what I know has not impressed me greatly and has not encouraged me to seek to know more.

M.R.:   But you met Michel Foucault, I believe, during a television broadcast in Amsterdam?

N.C.:   Yes, and we had some very good discussions before and during the broadcast. On Dutch television, we spoke for several hours, he in French and I in English; I don't know what the Dutch television viewers made of all that. We found ourselves in at least partial agreement, it seemed to me, on the question of "human nature," and perhaps not as much on politics (the two basic points about which Fons Elders interviewed us).

As far as the concept of human nature and its relation to scientific progress was concerned, it seemed that we were "climbing the same mountain, starting from opposite directions," to repeat a simile which Elders suggested. In my view, scientific creativity depends on two facts: on the one hand, on an intrinsic property of mind, and on the other, on a combination of social and intellectual conditions. There is no question of choosing between these. In order to understand a scientific discovery, it is necessary to understand the interaction between these factors. But personally I am more interested in the first, while Foucault stresses the second.

Foucault considers the scientific knowledge of a given epoch to be like a *grid* of social and intellectual conditions, like a system the rules of which permit the creation of new knowledge. In his view, if I understand him correctly, human knowledge is transformed due to social conditions and social struggles, with one grid replacing the other, thus bringing new possibilities to science. He is, I believe, skeptical about the possibility or the legitimacy of an attempt to place important sources of human knowledge within the human mind, conceived in an ahistorical manner.

His position also involves a different usage of the term *creativity*. When I speak of creativity in this context, I am not making a value judgment: creativity is an aspect of the ordinary and daily use of language and of human action in general. However, when Foucault speaks of creativity he is thinking more of the achievements of a Newton, for example—although he stresses the common social and intellectual base for the creations of scientific imagination, rather than the achievements of an individual genius—that is to say, he is thinking of the conditions for radical innovation. His use of the term is a more normal one than mine. But even if contemporary science may find some solution to problems relating to ordinary, normal creativity—and I am rather skeptical even about this—still it cannot hope, certainly, to be able to come to grips with true creativity in the more usual sense of the word, or, say, to foresee the achievements of great artists or the future discoveries of science. That seems a hopeless quest. In my opinion, the sense in which I am speaking of "normal creativity" is not unlike what Descartes had in mind when he made the distinction between a human being and a parrot. In the historical perspective of Foucault, one no longer seeks to identify the innovators and their specific achievement or the obstacles which stand in the way of the emergence of truth, but to determine how knowledge, as a system independent of individuals, modifies its own rules of formation.

M.R.:   In defining the knowledge of an epoch as a grid or system, doesn't Foucault draw near to structuralist thought, which also conceives of language as a system?

N.C.:   To reply properly it would be necessary to study this matter in depth. In any case, while I have been speaking of the limitations imposed on a class of accessible theories—linked to the limitations of the human mind that permit the construction of rich theories in the first place—he is more interested in the proliferation of theoretical possibilities resulting from the diversity of social conditions within which human intelligence can flourish.

M.R.:   In the same way, structuralist linguistics stresses the differences between languages.

N.C.:   I have to be cautious in response, because the expression "structural linguistics" can cover a great variety of positions. It is certainly true that American "neo-Bloomfieldian" linguists, who sometimes call themselves "structuralists," have been impressed above all by the diversity of languages, and that some of them, like Martin Joos, have gone so far as to declare, as a general proposition of linguistic science, that languages can differ from one another in an arbitrary manner. When they speak of "universals," this involves a characterization of a very limited nature, perhaps some statistical observations. On the other hand, such a characterization would be very wide of its mark in the case of other schools of structural linguistics; for example, the work of Roman Jakobson, who has always been concerned with linguistic universals which narrowly constrain the class of possible languages, especially in phonology.

As far as Foucault is concerned, as I've said, he seems skeptical about the possibility of developing a concept of "human nature" that is independent of social and historical conditions, as a well-defined biological concept. I don't believe that he would characterize his own approach as "structuralist." I don't share his skepticism. I would be in agreement with him in saying that human nature is not as yet within the range of science. Up to the present, it has escaped the reach of scientific inquiry; but I believe that in specific domains such as the study of language, we can begin to formulate a significant concept of "human nature," in its intellectual and cognitive aspects. In any case, I would not hesitate to consider the faculty of language as part of human nature.

M.R.: Did you and Foucault speak of the Port-Royal *Grammaire Générale*?

N.C.: More precisely, about my relationship to the work on the history of ideas. There are a number of misunderstandings on this subject.

These questions can be approached in various ways. My approach to the early modern rationalist tradition, for example, is not that of a historian of science or of philosophy. I have not attempted to reconstruct in an exhaustive manner what people thought at that time, but rather to bring to light certain important insights of the period that have been neglected, and often seriously distorted, in later scholarship, and to show how at that time certain persons had already discerned important things, perhaps without being fully aware of it. These specific intentions are spelled out quite explicitly in my book *Cartesian Linguistics,* for example.

I was interested in earlier stages of thought and speculation relating to questions of contemporary significance. And I tried to show in what ways and to what extent similar ideas were formulated, anticipations of later developments, perhaps from rather different perspectives. I think that we can often see, from our current vantage point in the progress of understanding, how a thinker of the past was groping toward certain extremely significant ideas, frequently in a very constructive and remarkable manner, and perhaps with only a partial awareness of the nature of his quest.

Let me offer an analogy. I am not proceeding in the manner of an art historian so much as that of an art lover, a person who looks for what has value to him in the seventeenth century, for example, that value deriving in large measure from the contemporary perspective with which he approaches these objects. Both types of approach are legitimate. I think it is possible to turn toward earlier stages of scientific knowledge, and by virtue of what we know today, to shed light on the significant contributions of the period in a way in which the most creative geniuses could not, because of the limitations of their time. This was the nature of my interest in Descartes, for example, and in the philosophical tradition that he influenced, and also Humboldt, who would not have considered himself a Cartesian: I was interested in his effort to make sense of the concept of free creativity based on a system of internalized rules, an idea that has certain roots in Cartesian thought, I believe.

The kind of approach I was taking has been criticized, but not on any rational grounds, so far as I can see. Perhaps I should have discussed the nature and legitimacy of such an approach in more detail, though it seemed to me (and still seems to me) obvious. What I have been saying is quite familiar in the history of science. For example, Dijksterhuis, in his major work on the origins of classical mechanics, points out, with reference to Newton, that "Properly speaking, the whole system can only be understood in the light of the subsequent development of the science."[1] Suppose that the insights of classical mechanics had been lost, and there had been a reversion to something more akin to "natural history"—the accumulation and organization of large amounts of data and phenomenal observations, perhaps a kind of Babylonian astronomy (though even this reference is probably unfair). Then suppose that in some new phase of science, questions similar to those of the period of classical mechanics had reemerged. It would then have been entirely appropriate, quite important in fact, to try to discover significant insights of an earlier period and to determine in what ways they were anticipations of current work, perhaps to be understood properly in the light of subsequent developments. This it seems to me is more or less what happened in the study of language and mind, and I think it is quite interesting to recover insights that have long been neglected, approaching earlier work (which has often been grossly misrepresented, as I showed) from the standpoint of current interests and trying to see how questions discussed in an earlier period can be understood, and sometimes reinterpreted, in the light of more recent understanding, knowledge, and technique. This is a legitimate approach, not to be confused with efforts (like those of Dijksterhuis in physics) to reconstruct exactly how the issues appeared and how ideas were constructed at an earlier time. Of course, one must be careful not to falsify earlier discussion, but I am aware of no critical analysis of my work that shows this to be the case. There has, I am sorry to say, been a good deal of outright misrepresentation of what I wrote, in what is called "the scholarly literature," and I have been surprised to find sharp criticism of my alleged views even on topics that I did not discuss at all. I have commented occasionally on some of these falsifications, as have others, but by no means exhaustively, and I won't pursue it here.

Any person engaged in intellectual work can do the same thing with himself: you can try to reconsider what you understood twenty years ago, and thus see in what direction, in a confused manner, you were striving to go, toward what goal that perhaps became clear and intelligible only much later ...

M.R.: What were the political disagreements between you and Foucault?

N.C.:   For my part, I would distinguish two intellectual tasks. One is to imagine a future society that conforms to the exigencies of human nature, as best we understand them; the other, to analyze the nature of power and oppression in our present societies. For him, if I understand him rightly, what we can imagine now is nothing but a product of the bourgeois society of the modern period: the notions of justice or of "realization of the human essence" are only the inventions of our civilization and result from our class system. The concept of justice is thus reduced to a pretext advanced by a class that has or wants to have access to power. The task of a reformer or revolutionary is to gain power, not to bring about a more just society. Questions of abstract justice are not posed, and perhaps cannot even be posed intelligibly. Foucault says, again if I understand him correctly, that one engages in the class struggle to win, not because that will lead to a more just society. In this respect I have a very different opinion. A social struggle, in my view, can only be justified if it is supported by an argument—even if it is an indirect argument based on questions of fact and value that are not well understood—which purports to show that the consequences of this struggle will be beneficial for human beings and will bring about a more decent society. Let us take the case of violence. I am not a committed pacifist, and thus do not say that it is wrong to use violence in all circumstances, say in self-defense. But any recourse to violence must be justified, perhaps by an argument that it is necessary to remedy injustice. If a revolutionary victory of the proletariat were to lead to putting the rest of the world into crematoria, then the class struggle is not justified. It can only be justified by an argument that it will bring an end to class oppression, and do so in a way that accords with fundamental human rights. Complicated questions arise here, no doubt, but they should be faced. We were in apparent disagreement, because where I was speaking of justice, he was speaking of power. At least, that is how the difference between our points of view appeared to me.[2]

CHAPTER 4

Empiricism and Rationalism

M.R.:   On many occasions you have criticized philosophic and scientific empiricism. Can you state your objections more precisely?

N.C.:   In a sense, empiricism has developed a kind of mind-body dualism, of a quite unacceptable type, just at the time when, from another point of view, it rejected such dualism. Within an empiricist framework, one approaches the study of the body as a topic in the natural sciences, concluding that the body is constructed of varied and specialized organs which are extremely complex and genetically determined in their basic character, and that these organs interact in a manner which is also determined by human biology. On the other hand, empiricism insists that the brain is a tabula rasa, empty, unstructured, uniform at least as far as cognitive structure is concerned. I don't see see any reason to believe that; I don't see any reason to believe that the little finger is a more complex organ than those parts of the human brain involved in the higher mental faculties; on the contrary, it is not unlikely that these are among the most complex structures in the universe. There is no reason to believe that the higher mental faculties are in some manner dissociated from this complexity of organization.

One can say that the dualism introduced by empiricist dogma is methodological rather than substantive. That is to say, it is taken for granted that the body must be studied by the ordinary methods of science, but in the case of the mind certain preconceptions have been imposed which have virtually removed this study from the domain of scientific inquiry. In fact, this dogmatism seems to be even more striking in the most recent period. Hume, for example, really did his best to show that his elementary principles concerning the acquisition of human knowledge were sufficient to cover an interesting class of cases and challenged his opponents to produce a legitimate "idea" that could not be derived from sense impression by his principles. There is a certain kind of ambiguity in his procedure here, since in part he seems to be engaged in a kind of scientific inquiry, trying to show that certain principles he proposed were in fact adequate to cover the crucial cases, while at other times he relies on these principles to demonstrate that some notion is "illegitimate," since it cannot be derived by them—an argument that rests on our accepting his not very plausible principles concerning the nature of the mind. Hume regarded the principle of inductive reasoning as a kind of "animal instinct," which would appear to be an empirical assumption. In modern versions, his assumptions have often been converted into dogma presupposed without serious effort to show them to be valid, or to reply to classical criticisms that were raised against these principles.

There is no reason to believe today that Hume's principles or anything resembling them are adequate to account for our "ideas" or our knowledge and beliefs, nor to think that they have any particular significance. There is no place for any a priori doctrine concerning the complexity of the brain or its uniformity as far as the higher mental functions are concerned. We must proceed to the investigation of the diverse cognitive structures developed normally by human beings in the course of their maturation and their relation to the physical and social environment, seeking to determine, as best we can, the principles which govern these cognitive structures. Once a certain understanding of the nature of these systems has been obtained, then we can reasonably study the basis on which they are acquired. In my opinion, the little that we know about these questions suggests that the mind, like the body, is in effect a system of organs—we could call them "mental organs" by analogy—that is to say, highly specific systems organized according to a genetic program that determines their function, their structure, the process of their development, in quite a detailed manner; the particular realization of these fundamental principles naturally depends on their interaction with the environment, as in the case of the visual system which we mentioned previously. If that is correct, the mind is a complex system of interacting faculties, which do not develop by means of uniform principles of "general intelligence"; it is constituted of "mental organs" just as specialized and differentiated as those of the body.

M.R.: It is for that reason, doubtless, that you insist on the autonomy of grammar, on the fact that grammatical structures do not depend on other cognitive systems. Does it seem impossible to you to think of language and the structure of knowledge in terms of the same model?

N.C.: I have nothing against comparisons, but I wonder whether we are likely to learn very much by proceeding in this direction. Note that one never tends toward that kind of proposal in physiology; no one suggests that we study the structure of the eye and the heart, and then search for analogies between them. One does not expect to find meaningful analogies. If the mind consists of a system of "mental organs," in interaction, certainly, but fundamentally different in their structure, we need not expect to find fruitful analogies among them.

To make myself clear, I am not about to propose all this as a new dogma, to replace empiricist doctrine. On the contrary, just as in studying the body, we must simply retain an open mind on this subject. We know a little about a number of cognitive systems, language being the most interesting case at the moment. That small degree of insight seems to me to suggest the preceding conclusions. The important thing, of course, is to determine the deeper principles and the detailed structure of various cognitive systems, their modes of interaction, and the general conditions which each system satisfies. If one finds that these systems are acquired in a uniform manner with very little specific structure, very well. But for the present at least it seems to me that quite different conclusions are indicated. That is what I mean when I say that one need not expect to find analogies.

M.R.:   Nor phenomena of interdependence. However, certain psychologists assert that perception exerts an influence on the potential structure of sentences. An essential aspect of your critique of empiricism is the rationalist hypothesis: the structure of the brain is determined a priori by the genetic code, the brain is programmed to analyze experience and to construct knowledge out of that experience. That may seem shocking . . .

N.C.:   I don't see anything shocking in that proposition. In physiology no one has ever accepted anything analogous to empiricist dogma with regard to the mind. No one finds it outlandish to ask the question: What genetic information accounts for the growth of arms instead of wings? Why should it be shocking to raise similar questions with regard to the brain and mental faculties? We are back to the methodological dualism of the empiricists.

M.R.:   That position does not suit contemporary "human sciences."

N.C.:   Especially not behaviorist psychology, or perhaps even Piaget, though his position seems to me obscure in crucial respects. Piaget considers himself to be an anti-empiricist; but some of his writings suggest to me that he is mistaken in this conclusion. Piaget develops a certain "constructive interactionism": new knowledge is constructed through interaction with the environment. But the fundamental question is evaded: *How* is this knowledge constructed, and why *just this kind* of knowledge and not some other? Piaget does not give any intelligible answer, as far as I can make out. The only answer that

I can imagine is to suppose an innate genetic structure which determines the process of maturation. Insofar as he considers it wrong to give such an answer, he falls back into something like the empiricism that he wants to reject. What he postulates is nowhere near sufficient, it seems to me, to account for the specific course of cognitive development.

That is not to deny the very great importance of the research that has been conducted by Piaget and his group at Geneva; it has opened up entirely new perspectives in the study of human knowledge. It is primarily the interpretation of their results which seems extremely doubtful to me, in particular their attitude toward what Piaget calls "innéisme," which seems to me altogether wrong.

In philosophy, the same problems appear in some of the work of Quine, for example.[1] At times he asserts that theories are developed by induction, which he identifies with conditioning. At other times he says the opposite: theories are not determined solely by conditioning or induction, but involve abstract hypotheses ultimately originating from some innate capacity.

In recent years he has oscillated between these two positions.[2]

Functionalism

M.R.:   The tendency of thought which has fought hardest against the independence of grammar as a "mental organ" is without doubt functionalism. It tends to explain the form of language by attributing a determining role to its function. This function is presumed to be *communication:* everything in language must contribute to communication, to a better communication, and inversely, nothing is linguistic which does not contribute to communication. Isn't that a fairly accurate portrait?

N.C.:   Functionalism holds that the use of language influences its form. This might be understood as a variant of empiricist doctrine about language learning, one that makes very little sense, as far as I can see. But we might understand the fundamental ideas quite differently. For example, George Miller and I suggested about fifteen years ago that there may be a "functional explanation" for the organization of language with grammatical transformations, which would be a well-designed system corresponding to a certain organization of short- and long-term memory, for example.

If one could demonstrate that, it would be interesting. But what does that mean basically? What would the analogous observation mean for some physical organ, say the heart? To be sure, the heart has a function: to pump blood. One may sensibly say that the structure of the heart is determined by that function. But suppose we ask the ontogenetic question: How does our heart become what it is? How does it grow in the individual from the embryo to its final form in the mature organism? The answer is not functional: the heart does not develop in the individual because it would be useful to carry out a certain function, but rather because the genetic program determines that it will develop as it does.

Every organ has certain functions, but these functions do not determine the ontogenetic development of the organism. Nobody would suggest that a group of cells decides that perhaps it would be a good idea to become a heart because such an organ is necessary to pump blood. If this group of cells becomes a heart, it is due to the information present in the genetic code, which determines the structure of the organism.

There is a place for functional explanation, but it is on the level of evolution. It is possible that a heart develops in the course of evolution in order to satisfy a certain function. Of course, I'm simplifying enormously. But this is a point that is useful to keep in mind: functional explanation does not relate to the way organs develop in the individual.

Let's go back to linguistics: here comparable remarks can be made. To my knowledge, no functional principle with very great plausibility has yet been proposed. But suppose that someone proposes a principle which says: The form of language is such-and-such because having that form permits a function to be fulfilled—a proposal of this sort would be appropriate at the level of evolution (of the species, or of language), not at the level of acquisition of language by an individual, one would suppose.

M.R.: As a consequence, insofar as your linguistics is a theory of language *and* of the acquisition of language by an individual, functionalism cannot be retained as a fundamental principle. Inversely, one might note that the legitimacy of the dependency relation between function and structure is not even a problem for functionalist linguists, because their aim is not to explain the acquisition of language but to *describe* a linguistic corpus.

N.C.: I doubt that functionalist linguists would accept that characterization. If they mean that ontogenetic development is directed by functional considerations, that seems just as plausible to me as suggesting that the development of the heart in the individual is guided by the utility of having an organ that pumps blood, and about as well supported by the factual evidence. Or, they might say that questions touching on the basis of language acquisition do not concern them. The crucial point, however, seems to me to be that there is no real debate about the validity of functionalism at the generally vague level on which we discuss the hypothetical evolution of the species, or in the study of language change; and there is no sensible way to invoke functional notions as explanatory concepts at the synchronic or ontogenetic level, so far as I can see.

It also seems to me important to avoid a certain vulgarization with respect to the use of language. There is no reason to believe —to repeat myself once again—that language "essentially" serves instrumental ends, or that the "essential purpose" of language is "communication," as is often said, at least if we mean by "communication" something like transmitting information or inducing belief. Someone who claims that this is *the* essential purpose of language must explain just what he means by it, and why he believes this function, and no other, to be so uniquely significant.

Language is used in many different ways. Language can be used to transmit information, but it also serves many other purposes: to establish relations among people, to express or clarify thought, for play, for creative mental activity, to gain understanding, and so on. In my opinion, there is no reason to accord privileged status to one or the other of these modes. Forced to choose, I would have to say something quite classical and rather empty: language serves essentially for the expression of thought.

I know of no reason to suppose that instrumental ends, or transmission of information about one's beliefs, or other actions that might reasonably be called "communication" (unless, of course, the term is used quite vacuously), have some unique significance compared with other characteristic uses of language. In fact, what is meant by the assertion that such-and-such is *the* goal of language, or its essential purpose, is far from clear.

Once again, this plurality of modes is characteristic of the most banal and normal use of language.

It is hard to know just what people mean when they say that language is "essentially" an instrument of communication. If you press them a bit and ask them to be more precise, you will often find, for example, that under "communication" they include communication with oneself. Once you admit that, the notion of communication loses all content; the expression of thought becomes a kind of communication. These proposals seem to be either false, or quite empty, depending on the interpretation that is given, even with the best of will. It is all so vague that discussion remains mystifying. I have no idea why such proposals are so often made, frequently with such fervor, or what on earth they are supposed to signify.

The real question is: How does this organism function, and what is its mental and physical structure?

M.R.: Empiricism (and, in particular, functionalism) has enjoyed an enormous success. In spite of all the demonstrations that have been made of its errors, today it still remains the dominant philosophy. To what do you attribute that success, that power to survive? To a conjunction of ideology and politics?

N.C.: On that point we must be careful, because here we enter into speculation. When certain ideas are dominant, it is very reasonable to ask why. The reason could be that they are plausibly regarded as true, they have been verified, etc. But in the case where they are without empirical foundations, and have little initial plausibility, the question arises more sharply: the answer may actually lie in the domain of ideology. Of course the argument here must be indirect, because we don't have any direct means of determining the ideological basis for the acceptance gained by a certain doctrine.

Perhaps the instrumentalist conception of language is related to the general belief that human action and its creations, along with the intellectual structure of human beings, are designed for the satisfaction of certain physical needs (food, well-being, security, etc.). Why try to reduce intellectual and artistic achievement to elementary needs?

Is the attraction of the several variants of empiricist doctrine based on experimental verification? Hardly. There is no such verification. Does it derive from their explanatory power? No, because they can explain very little. Is it due to some analogy to other systems about which we know more? No. Again, the systems known to biology are totally different. Animal intelligence seems to be quite different. So too the physical structures of the human organism. The rational hypotheses which we can propose to explain the dominance of empiricist doctrines do not apply.

It should be noted that empiricist doctrine has not merely been "accepted" for a long period, it was hardly even questioned, but rather simply assumed, tacitly, as the framework within which thinking and research must proceed.

Perhaps, then, some sociological factor might explain in a natural way why this point of view has been so widely adopted. We can ask ourselves, who accepts and disseminates these doctrines? Essentially, the intelligentsia, including scientists and non-scientists. What is the social role of the intelligentsia? As I have said, it has been quite characteristically manipulation and social control in all its varied forms. For example, in those systems called "socialist," the technical intelligentsia belong to the élite that designs and propagates the ideological system and organizes and controls the society, a fact that has long been noted by the non-Bolshevik left. Walter Kendall, for example, has pointed out that Lenin, in such pamphlets as *What Is To Be Done?*, conceived of the proletariat as a tabula rasa upon which the "radical" intelligentsia must imprint a socialist consciousness. The metaphor is a good one. For the Bolsheviks, the radical intelligentsia must bring a socialist consciousness to the masses from the outside; as Party members, the intelligentsia must organize and control society in order to bring "socialist structures" into existence.

This set of beliefs corresponds very well to the demands of the technocratic intelligentsia: it offers them a very important social role. And in order to justify such practices, it is very useful to believe that human beings are empty organisms, malleable, controllable, easy to govern, and so on, with no essential need to struggle to find their own way and to determine their own fate. For that empiricism is quite suitable. So from this point of view, it is perhaps no surprise that denial of any "essential human nature" has been so prominent in much of left-wing doctrine.

Analogously, the modern intelligentsia in the capitalist societies—that of the United States, for example—have a certain access to prestige and power by serving the state. So, much the same is true for the liberal intelligentsia in the West. Service to the state includes social manipulation, preservation of capitalist ideology and capitalist institutions, within the framework of state capitalism. In this case as well, the concept of an empty organism is useful. It is plausible that statist ideologues and administrators are attracted by this doctrine because it is so convenient for them, in eliminating any moral barrier to manipulation and control.

These remarks apply only for the last century, more or less. Before that the situation is rather different. Without doubt, at an earlier period empiricism was associated with progressive social doctrine, in particular, with classical liberalism; although, as we were discussing, that was not always the case. One may recall the ideas of the young Marx, who was far from empiricist doctrine in spirit. Why this link between progressive social thought and empiricist doctrine? Perhaps because empiricism seemed to have—and in a certain way did have—progressive social implications in contrast to reactionary and determinist doctrines, according to which the existing social structures, slavery, autocracy, the feudal hierarchy, the role of women, were founded on unchanging human nature. Against that doctrine, the idea that human nature is a historical product had a progressive content, as it also did, one might argue, throughout the early period of capitalist industrialization.

The determinist doctrines in question maintained that certain people were born to be slaves, by their very nature. Or consider the oppression of woman, which was also founded on such concepts. Or wage labor: willingness to rent oneself through the market is considered one of the fundamental and immutable human properties, in a version of the "human essence" characteristic of the era of capitalism.

In the face of such doctrines as these, it is natural for advocates of social change to adopt the extreme position that "human nature" is a myth, nothing but a product of history. But that position is incorrect. Human nature exists, immutable except for biological changes in the species.

M.R.: But that is not the same definition of human nature, it is no longer a matter of defining a psychology of individual character.

N.C.: Certainly, we can distinguish between theories that assign a determinate social status to particular individuals or groups by virtue of their alleged intrinsic nature (e.g., some are born to be slaves), and theories that hold that there are certain biological constants characteristic of the species, which may, of course, assume very different forms as the social and material environment varies. There is much to be said about all of these matters. It seems to me that one might suggest, in a very speculative manner, that such factors as the ones I have mentioned entered into the success of empiricism among the intelligentsia. I have discussed this question a bit in *Reflections on Language,* stressing the crucial and sometimes overlooked point that speculation about these matters of ideology is quite independent of the validity of the specific doctrines in question; it is when doctrines of little merit gain wide and unquestioned credence that such speculations as these become particularly appropriate.

In *Reflections,* I also mentioned that even at the earliest stages it is not so obvious that empiricism was simply a "progressive" doctrine in terms of its social impact, as is very widely assumed. There has been some interesting work in the past few years, for example, on the philosophical origins of racism, particularly by Harry Bracken, which suggests a much more complex history. It seems that racist doctrine developed in part as a concomitant of the colonial system, for fairly obvious reasons. And it is a fact that some leading empiricist philosophers (Locke, for example) were connected to the colonial system in their professional lives, and that racist attitudes were commonly advanced during this period by major philosophers, among others. It is perhaps not unreasonable to speculate that the success of empiricist beliefs, in some circles at least, might be associated with the fact that they offer a certain possibility for formulating racist doctrine in a way that is difficult to reconcile with traditional dualist concepts concerning "the human essence."

Bracken has suggested, plausibly it seems to me, that racist doctrine raises conceptual difficulties within the framework of dualist beliefs, that is, if they are taken seriously. Cartesian dualism raises what he has called "a modest conceptual barrier" to racist doctrine. The reason for that is simple. Cartesian doctrine characterizes humans as thinking beings: they are metaphysically distinct from non-humans, possessing a thinking substance *(res cogitans)* which is unitary and invariant—it does not have color, for example. There are no "black minds" or "white minds." You're either a machine, or else you're a human being, just like any other human being in essential constitution. The differences are superficial, insignificant: they have no effect on the invariant *human essence*.

I think it is not an exaggeration to see in Cartesian doctrine a conceptual barrier—a modest one, as Bracken carefully explains—against racism. On the other hand, the empiricist framework does not offer an analogous characterization of the human essence. A person is a collection of accidental properties, and color is one of them. It is thus somewhat easier to formulate racist beliefs in this framework, although it is not inevitable.

I don't want to exaggerate the importance of these speculations. But it is worth investigating the question whether colonial ideology did in fact exploit the possibilities made available by empiricist doctrine to formulate more easily the kind of racist beliefs that were employed to justify conquest and oppression. It is unfortunate that the carefully qualified speculations that have been proposed for investigation have evoked a rather hysterical response, and some outright falsification, on the part of a number of philosophers—who are, as Bracken has observed, quite willing to consider, and even advance, very explicit proposals concerning a possible relation between rationalism and various oppressive doctrines, racism among them, thus indicating that it is not the nature of the inquiry but rather its object that they consider intolerable.

I must emphasize again that these speculations, or any others concerning the ideological or social factors that contribute to the success of any doctrine, must be recognized for what they are: speculations which are at best suggestive. Again, questions of this kind arise especially when a doctrine enjoys a great deal of attraction and success among the intelligentsia in spite of little factual support or explanatory value. This is the case with empiricism, in my opinion.

M.R.:   Empiricism thus finds support both from the right and the left . . . That explains why generative grammar is often attacked by the progressive intelligentsia, precisely because of your reference to the hypothesis of "innate ideas," as it is called, that is, the genetic limitations imposed on language. This hypothesis is accused of idealism.

N.C.:   That is true, as you say. But the characterization is quite irrational. A consistent materialist would consider it as self-evident that the mind has very important innate structures, physically realized in some manner. Why should it be otherwise? As I have already mentioned, if we assume that human beings belong to the biological world, then we must expect them to resemble the rest of the biological world. Their physical constitution, their organs, and the principles of maturation are genetically determined. There is no reason for supposing the mental world to be an exception. The hypothesis which naturally comes to mind is that these mental systems, unusual in the biological world because of their extraordinary complexity, exhibit the general characteristics of known biological systems.

I would emphasize once again that even qualitative considerations of the most evident kind suggest this conclusion: it is difficult to see any other explanation for the fact that extremely complicated and intricate structures are acquired, in a like manner among all individuals, on the basis of very limited and often imperfect data.

M.R.:   Certain psychologists still are trying to make apes talk; as a result, they deny the qualitative difference between human beings and animals, a difference which you have adopted from Cartesianism and restated in the light of modern biology. Do those who are opposed to "innéism" take the same position as these psychologists?

N.C.:   I don't want to speak for others. Let's consider this question of human uniqueness. Imagine a Martian scientist who studies human beings from the outside, without any prejudice. Suppose that he has a great deal of time at his disposal, say, thousands of years. He notices immediately that there exists on earth a unique organism, whose conditions of life change considerably without corresponding changes in his constitution; that is, modern man. Apes and monkeys live as they lived millions of years ago, while human life changes radically and very rapidly. It is extremely varied, yet there is no corresponding diversity within the human species. Take a child from a Stone Age culture and raise him in New York: he will become a New Yorker. Raise an American baby in New Guinea, and he will become a Papuan "native." The genetic differences one finds are superficial and trivial, but human beings have the extraordinary characteristic of being able to live in very different ways. Human beings have history, cultural evolution, and cultural differentiation. Any objective scientist must be struck by the qualitative differences between human beings and other organisms, as much as by the difference between insects and vertebrates. If not, he is simply irrational.

Take an even more elementary criterion: proliferation. In that regard human beings are a species with remarkable biological success. Perhaps not if you compare them to insects—or chickens (but here the proliferation in fact results from human intervention)—but compared to higher organisms, monkeys or chimpanzees, for example, they are much more numerous. Thus, in the most elementary respects, human beings are quite different. No scientist could fail to see that.

Even the most superficial observation suffices to show that there are qualitative differences between humans and other complex organisms which must be explained. If our hypothetical Martian observer searches a bit further, he will find that human beings are unique in many respects, one of these being their ability to acquire a rich and varied linguistic system, which can be used freely and in the most subtle and complicated ways, merely by immersion in a linguistic community in which the system is used. It seems to me that a rational observer would conclude that specific qualities of "intelligence," proper to this species, must be assumed. If he is of an inquiring mind and enterprising, he will seek to determine the genetically fixed mental structures which underlie the unique achievements of this species.

M.R.:   I believe the rejection of "innate ideas" also springs from their association with the Cartesian notion of *soul* (âme) . . .

N.C.:   That may well be true. But consider this ancient problem of the human soul in its historical context. For Descartes, for example, the existence of the soul is assumed in quite a rational way as a scientific principle. In some respects his argument for the existence of the soul is not very different from Newton's argument for gravity, as a force of nature. Descartes was wrong, no doubt, but his procedure in itself was not at all unreasonable.

To see this, it is sufficient to pursue the analogy to Newton, though I don't want to exaggerate its importance. Newton showed that Cartesian mechanics could not account for the movement of heavenly bodies. To explain this movement he postulated a new force: gravity, attraction at a distance; that is, a force which by the criteria of his time was considered to be occult, mystical, because action at a distance violated basic assumptions of mechanics. Newton showed that in this way one could account for the facts, though he too was quite uncomfortable with the "occult force" he was postulating. This postulate became the common sense of following generations, with Laplace and others. An inconceivable idea for pre-Newtonian physics subsequently became part of science because of its remarkable explanatory power.

For his part, Descartes believed—wrongly—that "push-pull" mechanics could explain all phenomena of the natural world, except such things as consciousness and human creativity. Thus to explain what was beyond the scope of his mechanics, he postulated another substance; little else was open to him, given the metaphysics of substance and accident to which he was committed. One can now imagine all sorts of other things, which are not part of his mechanics. But let us suppose that Descartes or the Cartesians could have gone further and invented a mathematics of the mind, a successful explanatory theory. Then their belief would have become part of the science of subsequent generations, like the physics of Newton.

To repeat, the existence of the soul, Descartes's second substance, is a scientific proposition: it is false, but it is not irrational. Had he elaborated his theory of the soul to an explanatory theory, he might have created a new science to supplement his speculative physiology. He was completely right to propose new principles and to seek out their consequences.

One might say that Descartes's belief that the soul is a simple substance which cannot be analyzed created an obstacle to the development of an explanatory theory of the mind, a theory which in principle might be assimilated to a suitably extended physics—but that is an altogether different question.

A convincing rejection of his dualism requires a demonstration that his postulate is useless, or unnecessary because we can explain the properties of the human mind in other ways. Let us then look for such an explanation . . . It might turn out that we are led to new principles when we inquire into the nature of the mind. It is conceivable, though not demonstrated, that principles entirely different from those of contemporary physics enter into the explanation of mental phenomena. In all these matters one must guard against dogmatism.

M.R.:   To make precise what you are opposing to empiricism, I think it is important to remember that for you the mental organ is that which corresponds to the *grammar* and not to the language. The structuralists think that one memorizes extended sentences, that is to say, the language (de Saussure's *langue*), and that this represents the grammar. But for you, what is constructed in memory as grammar is quite another thing. It is necessary to insist on this difference because so often the set of rules which makes the sentences of a language possible is confused with the language as a set of memorized sequences.

For de Saussure, on the contrary, it was the language—
langue—which was deposited in memory. He could not distinguish the memory which we can have of this or that extended
sentence from the "memory"—of the grammatical form. The
situation is quite different here. The two kinds of memory are
different. The construction of the grammar is due to the language faculty. But don't you think that another confusion can
arise because of the ambiguity of the English word *language*
(both *langue* and *langage*)? Therefore, one could understand
that it is the language as *langue* which is innate . . .

N.C.:   . . . Which would be absurd, of course; if French were
innate, I would speak it . . .

It is the mechanism of language acquisition that is innate. In
a given linguistic community, children with very different experience arrive at comparable grammars, indeed almost identical
ones, so far as we know. That is what requires explanation.
Even within a very narrow community—take the élite in Paris
—the experiences are varied. Each child has a different experience, each child is confronted by different data—but in the end
the system is essentially the same. As a consequence we have
to suppose that all children share the same internal constraints
which characterize narrowly the grammar they are going to
construct.

M.R.:   This hypothesis also explains why, when the moment of maturation is passed—adolescence—it is no longer
possible to learn a language; the wolf-children never learn to
speak, and we speak a foreign language which we have learned
late in life with an accent. Without these biological constraints,
foreign accent would be inexplicable.

N.C.:   Yes, there seems to be a critical age for learning a
language, as is true quite generally for the development of the
human body. Patterns of growth are determined genetically, for
example, sexual maturation, to take a case that occurs long
after birth. It would evidently be absurd to maintain that only
what one sees at birth is determined genetically.

Even death, to a certain degree, is genetically determined. To say that the genetically determined properties of an organism cannot manifest themselves before the appropriate conditions exist, and that in general the genetic program is spelled out in a way that is partly predetermined and partly influenced by environmental factors, is a virtual truism. In the study of physical development it is a commonplace, and once again, if the methodological dualism of empiricist dogma is abandoned, there is no reason to be surprised by the discovery of similar phenomena in the study of higher mental functions.

PART II

Generative Grammar

CHAPTER 5

The Birth of
Generative Grammar

Mitsou Ronat

The subject of this chapter is what distinguishes Chomsky's approach fundamentally from structuralism. Let us just briefly recall—in greatly simplified form—some properties of his generative model. A generative grammar, he says, must render explicit the implicit knowledge of the speaker, or the "intelligence" of the reader (the term intelligence *receives a special definition here). Even the most complete traditional grammars "forget" to mention the simplest characterizations. For example, with their instructions as the sole indication, one would have been unable to generate any of the above sentences. In French, nothing would prevent a priori the production of the sequence,* La grammaire est très générative *(The grammar is very generative) on the model of* La grammaire est très intéressante *(The grammar is very interesting), if we start with the definitions that the traditional French grammar of, say, Grevisse gives of the adjective. Grevisse did not specify this because the speaker of French "knows" intuitively that one does not say this. On the other hand, the French speaker must learn by heart the formation of the plural that distinguishes* loyal/loyaux *from* naval/navals; *those are irregularities ...*

Furthermore, Chomsky proposes the construction of a formal model. Starting from an axiom and a set of well-defined rules, the desired sequences are generated "mechanically." What was termed the base component *of the grammar was conceived in the beginning as a finite set of* rewriting rules, *that is, rules having the form* φ →ψ, *which can be translated as follows: Each time you encounter the element   , which is to the left of the arrow, you can replace it by ψ, which is to the right of the arrow. I will not go into further detail here, but see Adrian Akmajian and Frank Heny's* Introduction to the Principles of Transformational Syntax, *or C. L. Baker's* Introduction to Generative Transformational Syntax.[1]

I will, however, give an idea of what the base component of a grammar is with a very simple example. Imagine a language that has only three words: Jules, Chloe, *and* loves. *The speakers of this language know "spontaneously" that certain combinations (without repetition) of these three words belong to the language, while others do not; for example*

> * Jules Chloe loves
> OK Jules loves Chloe
> * loves Jules Chloe
> * loves Chloe Jules
> OK Chloe loves Jules
> * Chloe Jules loves

> where * = does not belong to the language;
> OK = belongs to the language

The problem is to render this "knowledge" explicit. One can propose the following grammar:

$$\{G\} \quad \left. \begin{array}{l} S \rightarrow N \; VP \\ VP \rightarrow V \; N \\ N \rightarrow \left\{ \begin{array}{l} Jules \\ Chloe \end{array} \right\} \\ V \rightarrow loves \end{array} \right\} = \left\{ \begin{array}{l} G = \text{grammar} \\ \text{"Sentence" is rewritten: noun + verb} \\ \quad \text{phrase} \\ \text{"Verb phrase" } (VP) \text{ is rewritten: verb +} \\ \quad \text{noun} \\ \text{"Noun" is rewritten: } Jules \text{ or } Chloe \\ \text{"Verb" is rewritten: } loves \end{array} \right.$$

Following these "deductions" mechanically (if S, *then* N + VP, *etc.), one will arrive at the desired sequences; furthermore, one can never deduce undesirable sequences. Let us construct a* derivation:

S is replaced by: *N VP*
Replacing *VP* by *V N: N V N*
Replacing the first *N* by Jules: *Jules V N*
Replacing *V* by *loves: Jules loves N*
Replacing the second *N* by *Chloe: Jules loves Chloe*
(One cannot go further, the string is terminal)

We can equally well represent the derivation by a tree or phrase marker. *This tree describes the structure of the terminal elements of the sentence. Thus, we see that the relation of* Jules *and of* Chloe *with respect to the verb is not symmetrical:*

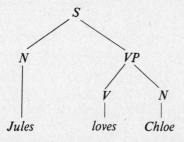

One can hardly doubt that the grammar of a natural language is incomparably more complicated. Chomsky has shown that rewriting rules, no matter how complex they may be, are not sufficient for describing the natural languages.

The grammar of a language is thus a model that must include several other components in addition to the rewriting rules of the base component. In his earliest writings, Chomsky showed that it is necessary to incorporate in the grammar at least two other levels. The rewriting rules give the structure of the sequences of words; it is necessary to add a morphophonological component and a transformational component. The transformational rules are rules of a different type, which transform the syntactic struc-

tures generated by the rewriting rules into other structures, according to precise principles. The relation between the active and the passive has usually been cited as an example involving transformation. *

The evolution of this theory has led to the complication of the model at certain points and to its simplification at others. Later, I will indicate the points at which the model has evolved.

The history of generative grammar seems to fall into three main periods, which successively have placed in the foreground one of the essential aspects of the new theory. The first, which lasted from the beginning of the 1950s to the middle of the 1960s, sought to make linguistics a science: physics seemed to be the model of reference. This is the period of The Logical Structure of Linguistic Theory *(or* LSLT, *as it will be cited).*

After that, from 1965 to 1970, the question of semantics became more central: must the meaning *of words and sentences be accounted for in the grammar, and if so, in what fashion? Very lively controversy accompanied the different answers given.*

Finally, after 1970, research became oriented more toward the problems posed by universal grammar. To comply with the formal exigencies of these discussions, I have asked Noam Chomsky to follow this thematic chronology.   M.R.

The History of Generative Grammar:
Opposition to Structuralism

M.R.:   Generative grammar is born of the break with and in opposition to structuralism. The latter, in general, conceived of linguistics as a classificatory activity. You have given the discipline a *logical structure,* a scientific structure . . .

N.C.:   The term *science* is perhaps honorific. My own inclination is to attach less importance to the precise description of some domain of linguistic data than to the explanatory power and depth of underlying principles.

---

*In French an example is the transformation which displaced *tous* in *Tous les garçons sont partis—Les garçons sont tous partis.* See Richard Kayne, *French Syntax* (Cambridge, Mass.: MIT Press, 1975).

I take for granted that in something as complex as the actual utilization of language and the judgments about language, many systems enter into interaction. No matter how careful our observations, how objective our methods, and how replicable our "experiments," the facts presented are, in my opinion, of little interest in themselves. What is of interest is their bearing on explanatory theories that seek to formulate the fundamental principles of the language faculty. Speaking just for myself, organizing the "facts of language" does not interest me very much. The notion "facts of language" has little sense outside of at least an implicit theory of language. One can perfectly well have different interests; I am simply trying to make clear what interests me. Frankly, I do not believe that seeking to account for "all the facts" constitutes a reasonable goal. In contrast, what seems important to me is the discovery of facts that are crucial for determining underlying structure and abstract hidden principles. If such principles do not exist, the enterprise is not worth undertaking. If they do exist, then facts are interesting (to me, at least) insofar as they bear on the truth of these principles. The discovery of such facts is often a creative achievement in itself, and very much "theory-related." "The facts," in any interesting sense of that notion, are not simply presented to us, nor is it of great interest, in my opinion, to present "the facts" in an exact manner, although of course the *pertinent* facts (again a notion that is linked to theory) must be presented in as precise a manner as possible . . .

M.R.:   . . . as in physics.

N.C.:   . . . If you like. That is how it seems to me. At each stage in the development of physics there have been innumerable unexplained "facts," or facts that seemed totally incompatible with the theories being actively pursued. To take a classic example, consider the "facts" of sorcery or of astrology, which seemed very well established by the standards of empirical research in the period when classical Galilean physics became established scientific doctrine. Or to take a less exotic example, consider the problems encountered by seventeenth-century physics in dealing with observations by telescope, many of which were not understood until quite recently. Or simply the problem of explaining why the apparent size and brightness of the planets did not vary as predicted by Copernican theory, as the distance between the planets changes. Or consider Galileo's inability to explain why objects don't fly off the earth, if it is indeed revolving on its axis—the explanation only came later. Without going into a detailed discussion, it is certainly true that throughout the history of the serious sciences many problems in explaining facts were put aside, in the hope that they would be explained some day. To account for "all the facts" in the physical world has never been the goal of physics in the modern period, in the sense that some linguists think that a grammar must account for "all the facts" of language and the utilization of language. The great success of physics is due in part to the willingness to restrict attention to the facts that seem crucial at a particular level of understanding, and perhaps to look for quite exotic facts that will be crucial for the theory, without taking into account even evident facts when these do not seem pertinent to physical theory (and to be quite honest, sometimes even when they appear inconsistent with it).

As for those varieties of "structuralism" or of "descriptive linguistics" that are interested primarily in the arrangement of "facts," one can doubtless say that my own goals are not necessarily incompatible with theirs, but that we are dealing with different intellectual enterprises. In my *Logical Structure of Linguistic Theory,* which contains my doctoral thesis, I tried to discuss these questions.

I suggested there that for the purposes of linguistic theory, we should be concerned with certain phenomena that were pretty much excluded from the descriptive linguistics of that period: those facts relating to what has sometimes been called the "creative" use of language, conceived as *normal* usage of language. These facts have not been treated systematically by traditional grammar or by structural linguistics although, as I have frequently pointed out, they were a classical concern, for example, in work by Humboldt, Paul, Jespersen, and others.

The traditional grammars, even those of great scope like Jespersen's,[2] present innumerable examples of complex structures, but do not give explicit principles for determining that these structures—and others which somehow "resemble" them —belong to the language, while other imaginable structures do not.

In fact, this question was not really raised. Jespersen, I suppose, did not have the impression that there was something fundamental missing in his presentation, despite his recognition of the importance of what he called "free expressions." In presenting his innumerable examples he thought that he had given an account of the language, so it appears. In reality his commentaries were not sufficient, because they appealed implicitly to the "intelligence" of the reader—to understand them and to use these examples and his often insightful commentary in the creation and comprehension of new forms, the reader had to add his own intuitive knowledge of language.

Structural grammars did not undertake the task of studying a range of highly complex syntactic structures, as the traditional grammars did.

This contribution of the intelligent reader, presupposed by previous grammars, must be made explicit if we hope to discover the basic principles of language. This is the first goal of generative grammar. In psychological terms: What is the nature of the intuitive, unconscious knowledge, which (in particular) permits the speaker to use his language?

At the time that question had not been squarely faced, though it had occasionally been put forth, and it remains a serious question today, in many crucial respects an unanswered one.

The second goal is to construct an explanatory theory. We have an at least potential explanation when we can deduce certain phenomena from general principles, that is, when we can provide a deductive chain of reasoning departing from these principles, given certain particular facts considered as "boundary conditions."

To be more concrete, let us take a well-known example, the behavior of the English auxiliary system.*   One can, I think, explain some aspects of this system on the basis of a certain theory of transformational grammar and certain given facts: among them, the elementary examples of the auxiliary system in simple declarative sentences. Starting from these principles and empirical facts, I tried to show that one could explain the behavior of the auxiliary in a variety of constructions—interrogative, negative, and so on.

---

* The rules that deal with the behavior of the English auxiliary are quite complicated, but can be simplified by the use of transformations—See Syntactic Structures, *chapter 5.*

Starting with a rewriting rule (see above, p. 104) which describes the behavior of the declarative sentence, we have:

$Verb \rightarrow AUX + V$

$Aux \rightarrow C (M) (have + en) (be + ing) (be + en)$

where the elements in ( ) are optional;
where C corresponds either to a grammatical zero

element ϕ, or to an element S which belongs to the third person singular, or to the element *past;*
where M corresponds to *will, can, may, shall, must,* i.e., the English modals.

(There is furthermore an operation affix-movement, *which attaches the grammatical affixes* S, -en, -ing, ϕ, *etc., to the verbs that follow them: for example, the sequence* Aux + V *is rewritten first as* C + V, *then as* S + V, *and as result of* affix-movement, *one obtains* V + S; *thus* S + leave *is turned into* leave + S, *etc.)*

The negative transformation introduces the element not *after the second element of the* Aux *rule. If* M *is not realized, a transformation inserts the element* do, *giving* He didn't leave, *etc.*

The interrogative transformation inverts the subject noun phrase and the sequence C + (M): Will he leave?

If M *is missing,* do *is introduced as before:* Did they leave?

Thus the deep structure of negative and interrogative sentences resembles that of declarative sentences, and the same properties show up in other constructions as well. If we were to describe the phenomena directly without such rules as these, we would have a very complex system of rewriting rules and the basic regularities would remain unexpressed.

A third goal appeared clearly only later, at the end of the fifties (before that it was implicit). It had to do with considering the general principles of language as the properties of a biologically given system that underlies the acquisition of language. From this point of view, one might think of the "boundary conditions" as the facts encountered by someone who learns a language; what one tries to explain, then, is essentially the knowledge of the language attained by the speaker presented with such facts. To go back to the preceding example, if we assume that the speaker possesses as part of his biological make-up the general principles of transformational grammar, and is presented with some subset of the forms of the English auxiliary, then he would *know,* because he could deduce it, the behavior of these elements in other cases, that is, the other cases would follow from the simplest permissible rule compatible with the given cases. This, at least, is the general pattern of a possible explanation.

Thus my work sought to answer two questions: first, what is the system of linguistic knowledge that has been attained, and is internally represented, by a person who knows some language? And second, how can we account for the growth and attainment of such knowledge? The second question can be thought of in psychological terms—how can knowledge be acquired?—or alternatively as the question of how we explain the phenomena of language.

M.R.: When did you think for the first time of proposing an explanatory theory in linguistics?

N.C.: That was what interested me about linguistics in the first place. As an undergraduate at the University of Pennsylvania in the late 1940s I did an undergraduate thesis called "Morphophonemics of Modern Hebrew," later expanded to a master's thesis with the same title in 1951. That work, which has not been published, was a "generative grammar" in the contemporary sense; its primary focus was what is now called "generative phonology," but there was also a rudimentary generative syntax. I suppose one might say that it was the first "generative grammar" in the contemporary sense of the term. Of course there were classical precedents: Panini's grammar of Sanskrit is the most famous and important case, and at the level of morphology and phonology, there is Bloomfield's *Menomini Morphophonemics,* published only a few years earlier, though I did not know about it at the time. Anyway, the central part of this project was an attempt to demonstrate in painstaking detail that the generative grammar I presented was the "simplest possible" grammar in a well-defined technical sense: namely, given a certain framework for the formulation of rules and a precise definition of "simplicity," the grammar was "locally optimal" in the sense that any interchange of order of rules in a tightly ordered system of many rules would lead to a less simple grammar. Reading back into this work the explicit concerns of a later period, one might say, then, that the goal was to show exactly how this grammar with its empirical consequences would be constructed by someone initially equipped with the framework for rules and the definition of simplicity (the evaluation measure), and given a sufficient sample of the data. Actually, this was done in far greater detail and scale than anything I've attempted since, and was far too ambitious, I suppose.

That grammar did, as I said, contain a rudimentary generative syntax. The grammar associated phonetic representation with what we would now call "base-generated" syntactic structure. Parenthetically, this was a pre-transformational grammar. Harris's early work on transformations was then under way and as a student of his I was familiar with it, but I did not see then how this work could be recast within the framework of generative grammar that I was trying to work out. In place of transformations, the grammar had a complex system of indices assigned to syntactic categories, which indicated syntactic relations inexpressible within the framework of segmentation and classification that was later constructed, in somewhat different terms, as the theory of phrase structure grammar.

Since that time my major interest has been to make precise the basic principles which enter into the knowledge of language that has been attained by the speaker-hearer; and beyond that, to try to discover the general theoretical principles which account for the fact that this system of knowledge, rather than something else, develops in the mind when a person is placed in a certain linguistic environment. In a general way, I might say that I am still working very much within the framework of that early unpublished work. That is, I think the right approach to the fundamental theoretical issues is the one attempted there: to make precise a certain format and schematism for grammars, and to provide an evaluation procedure (or simplicity measure) that leads to the choice of a particular system, a particular grammar that is of the required form, namely, the optimal, most highly valued system of the required form that is compatible with the presented data. Then what the "language learner" comes to know is that most highly valued system; it is that system that underlies the actual use of language by the person who has gained this knowledge. I'll come back to this point.

I continued this early work in *The Logical Structure of Language Theory (LSLT)*—which was published in part only in 1975, twenty years after it was essentially completed. The psychological point of view did not begin to appear until the end of the fifties, especially with a very important review article by Lees written for *Language.* * This was a review of *Syntactic Structures,* which appeared in 1957, almost the same time as the book. In it Lees brought up the issue of language learning.

I wrote on similar questions in the years that followed, but we had been thinking about these issues for some time—Morris Halle[3] and Eric Lenneberg,[4] among others.

One of the things that most interested us was the critique of the behavioral sciences. We were trying to work out a rather

---

*See below, p. 133.

different approach to cognitive psychology. Little of this appears in *LSLT* because it seemed to me too audacious and premature. There is a more detailed discussion in the introduction to the 1975 edition of *LSLT.*

M.R.:   Your theoretical positions were accorded a mixed reception in linguistic circles . . . I remember reading review articles on the first colloquia in which you participated, the Texas Conference. The discussion was an epic confrontation. You opposed *evaluation procedures* (mechanisms that would tell which of two grammars, proposed to account for the facts, is the better one) to the *discovery procedures* of the structuralists, which were designed to construct the grammar directly from the facts.

N.C.: On this point one must distinguish carefully among the several tendencies that have been called "structuralist." American descriptive linguistics is one of these. Its chief contribution, in my opinion, was to raise for the first time a problem that one could readily interpret as that of explanation, or of the acquisition of language. What I mean is that the development of "discovery procedures" could have been understood as an approach to a theory of language acquisition, and also as an explanatory theory, considered from the dual perspective of psychology and epistemology. It is interesting to see that that was not the case; the linguists who were developing discovery procedures did not say: "Here is the corpus, the empirical conditions imposed by the data. Our discovery procedures constitute the theory which, applied to the corpus, produces the grammar. That grammar represents linguistic knowledge. In presenting this theory we have given an explanation for the fact that a speaker, having learned a language, knows this and that; the discovery procedure is part of his genetic equipment, and in applying it to the data of experience, he constructs this grammar, which represents his knowledge of language."

That would have been a reasonable way of interpreting what they were doing. But they did not give such an interpretation, for various reasons. However, that approach, implicit in their work, seems to me the most important contribution of this variety of structuralism. I repeat, this is not their interpretation. But I believe it to be legitimate as a reconstruction, even though it conflicts with what most of the people who did this work actually had in mind, to the best of my knowledge.

In work that I was doing in the late 1940s and early 1950s I tried to overcome some crucial deficiencies in the discovery procedures that had been developed and to make these procedures explicit, while assuming in the back of my mind a position concerning the so-called psychological reality of these procedures that was sharply in conflict with prevailing assumptions in the field, as I understood them, assumptions that might be called "fictionalist." It seems to have been generally assumed that the discovery procedures could be justified only in "pragmatic" terms, as providing an organization of the corpus that would be useful for one or another purpose. There were exceptions, for example, Charles Hockett, who put forth an explicitly "realistic" interpretation of discovery procedures in an important brief article in 1948, in the *International Journal of American Linguistics.* I was also taking for granted that the discovery procedures were basically true, in the sense that one might think of them as a representation of the procedures that were actually employed to provide the knowledge we have from the data we are given. For a long time I thought that the discovery procedures appearing in the literature were correct in their essentials—that is, that the methods employed by structural linguists like Zellig Harris,[5] with whom I was studying, were in principle correct, and that only some refinements were necessary to make them work. I spent quite a lot of time and energy, for about five or six years, I guess, trying to overcome some obvious defects of these procedures so that they would be able to produce a correct grammar with infinite descriptive scope from a finite corpus of the language; that, evidently, is the proper formulation of the task, if we think of these procedures as in effect a "learning theory" for human language.

There were thus two interrelated questions:

—Is it correct to give a psychological interpretation to these methods?

—Are these discovery procedures the ones which express correctly the biological given that makes the acquisition of language possible?

Note that we cannot properly pose the second question unless we accept a positive reply to the first. We cannot inquire into the "correctness" of methods without considering them to be an expression—more precisely, an intended expression—of some psychological reality. It is only under this "realist" interpretation that the question of correctness or truth arises. But again, this realist interpretation was not that of Harris and most others who had worked out the more elaborate procedures of analysis.

More and more I began to realize that the answer to the second question was negative. These procedures had insurmountable defects; they were wrong, in principle. The right approach seemed to involve principles that were more abstract, more indirect. I slowly came to believe that it was necessary to assume general principles, a general abstract schematism, which, when confronted with the given data, would yield a grammar representing linguistic knowledge, along the lines I mentioned earlier.

On the psychological level, structuralist discovery procedures correspond essentially to the empiricist view, according to which the acquisition of knowledge requires operations of classification and induction . . .

M.R.: It is in that sense that structural linguistics is linked to empiricism . . .

N.C.: In either the European version (with Troubetskoy,[6] who was quite concerned with these questions) or the American version, the procedures are essentially taxonomic, based on techniques of segmentation and classification that proceed gradually toward ever larger linguistic units.

The principles must be totally different—today I am convinced of that. One must begin by characterizing potential systems of knowledge with the help of principles which express the biological given. These principles determine the type of grammars that are available in principles. They are associated with an evaluation procedure which, given possible grammars, selects the best one. The evaluation procedure is also part of the biological given. The acquisition of language thus is a process of selection of the best grammar compatible with the available data. If the principles can be made sufficiently restrictive, there will also be a kind of "discovery procedure"—in some sense there must be such a "procedure," since knowledge is attained —but of a very different sort from what was contemplated in structuralist theory.

This conception of the nature of human knowledge, and particularly of language, is very different from the empiricist conception because one assumes the general form of the resulting system of knowledge to be given in advance. The system is not constructed gradually, step by step, by induction, segmentation and classification, generalization and abstraction, and so on.

Consequently, I think we might identify three fundamental issues that arise in comparing structuralist linguistics to generative grammar. First, with regard to the goal of explicit characterization of the attained linguistic knowledge. Second, the interpretation of the procedures: are the analytic procedures of B. Bloch,[7] of Harris, of Troubetskoy,[8] simply ways of organizing a corpus? Or do they constitute empirical hypotheses that are strong and interesting, with respect to psychological reality, and specifically to biologically given innate structure?

On this point work in generative grammar has characteristically taken a very explicit position. Yes, we propose such empirical hypotheses. Consequently, we consider pertinent all data that have any bearing on the validity of these hypotheses. At least in my opinion, it has always seemed evident that only the "realist" interpretation of linguistic theory, whether procedural or not, provides the basis for a significant discipline, one that is worth pursuing.

Trends in structuralist linguistics have varied on this question, and there are also some problems of interpretation. I believe that Jakobson and Troubetskoy did take a position close to that later adopted within generative grammar. They speak of psychological reality, it seems to me, as did Edward Sapir, for example, quite explicitly. Furthermore, at least in phonology, they postulated universal structural principles and even, in a sense, evaluation procedures in the form of considerations of symmetry, minimizing redundancy, and so on. Harris, on the contrary, rejected the realist psychological interpretation quite explicitly, at least in his early work—I am not sure that this is also true of his more recent work since the late sixties. In his *Methods* and other works up to the early sixties, he presented his theory as providing various alternatives for organizing data. The same is true of Bloch and others, though not of Hockett.

Finally, the third question deals with the nature of correct procedure. Is this a discovery procedure, inductive and taxonomic? Or is the proper approach of something like the rationalist type, that is, a characterization of the general form of knowledge (knowledge of language, in this case), with methods for choosing among alternative realizations of this general system under the empirical conditions given by experience?

I think it is proper to conceive of the theory of distinctive features in phonology and the various proposals concerning relative preference ("markedness") as a schema for a system of knowledge—if not an acquisition model. Though it is worth noting that Troubetskoy, in his phonological work, sought to furnish taxonomic procedures.

M.R.:   In relation to the second point, I've noted that there are many divergences over the definition given to the activity of linguists. The analyses, the theories they present, are these simply intellectual games or do they seek to establish the truth (even partially) of an objective law imposed upon something real?

N.C.:   The question is, how does one interpret a discovery

procedure? Is it solely a matter of organizing linguistic data, or a way of expressing a psychological reality?

It is interesting to look more closely at the *practice* of the linguists, who argued explicitly that they were simply providing techniques for compact organization of data. That practice rests upon a tacit belief to the contrary, and this holds throughout the entire development of structural linguistics. Constantly, whenever someone proposed a method or procedure, someone else would point out that this procedure leads to "undesirable results." Then certain corrections and improvements were proposed. In this way procedures were constantly refined.

But what meaning can we give to the notion "undesirable result"? There is no such notion, at least in any interesting sense, if all that is at stake is a way of organizing data; then there can only be results that are neither good nor bad, apart from minimal considerations of redundancy or consistency. One cannot be right or wrong in classifying data in a theoretical vacuum. Consequently, to the degree that one recognizes tacitly the existence of such notions as "good results" versus "unwanted results," it becomes evident that one is committed to some notion of psychological reality, that is, of truth, no matter how much the commitment is denied.

However, the explicit rejection of such a commitment makes it very difficult to arrive at such an interpretation of much of this work—which might find its rationale in this interpretation.

Two Definitions of Transformation

M.R.: The concept of "transformation" is a fundamental one in your theory. It is also one of its principal innovations. In your model, the transformational component operates on the "output" of the base component (the rewriting rules): it takes phrase structures (trees) and transforms them into other phrase structures (trees).*

---

*See the example given above, p. 110.

But the linguist Zellig Harris had already used the term *transformation*. The distinction between the two uses of the term has often been poorly understood. Could you state it precisely?

N.C.: Harris's concept of "transformation" was not strictly speaking "linguistic" in its origin—or, more precisely, not a concept that belongs to the theory concerned with the grammatical structure of sentences. Harris developed this concept as part of his study of discourse in the late 1940s. The linguistic theory he had presented in his *Methods* offered only tools for describing units that do not exceed the length of a single sentence. When he attempted to extend these methods to the structure of discourse, he observed at once that the methods of segmentation and classification devised for the grammar of sentences did not lead to any useful result. He therefore sought a way to reduce the set of complex sentences of discourse to a form in which they would be susceptible to analysis by the methods devised for sentences and their parts. He proposed the use of certain "transformations" to "normalize" the discourse, to transform complex sentences into uniform simple structures to which the methods of structural linguistics might apply: segmentation of sequences, substitution of elements, classification, and so on. For Harris, transformations were systematic relations between sentences, between "surface structures." Technically, a transformation in this sense is an unordered pair of linguistic structures, taken to be structurally equivalent in a certain sense. To give a concrete example, think of two linguistic structures, each on one side of a double arrow, each structure described by a succession of grammatical categories of which it is composed. Here is how one formulates the active-passive relation within this framework:

$$N_x V N_y \leftrightarrow N_y \text{ is } Ved \text{ by } N_x$$

which is read as:

Noun X + Verb + Noun Y is equivalent to
Noun Y + *is* + Verb in past participle + *by* + Noun X

The two structures on either side of the arrow in such formulas are held to be equivalent in the following sense: If we choose a particular noun (say *John*) for N_x and a particular noun (say *Mary*) for N_y and a particular verb (say *see*) for V, then the two substitution instances—that is, *John sees Mary* on the left and *Mary is seen by John* on the right—have the same degree of acceptability as sentences. Such "equivalences" can be used to normalize a discourse in the following manner: If we are given a sentence in a discourse in one of the two forms, then we can replace it by the corresponding sentence in the other form. By continuing to apply these equivalence transformations to a discourse, we can reduce the sentences to similar forms, to which the substitution procedures developed for the grammar of sentences can be applied, and we can construct substitution classes of words that play more or less the same role in discourse; these discourse categories must not be confused with the lexical or phrase categories of the language. This is the basic idea of "discourse analysis," as Harris has developed it in various publications since about 1950. What is relevant in this context is that transformational relations in Harris's sense were developed in the course of an attempt to extend structural methods to the analysis of discourse.

On the theoretical level, one essential characteristic of Harris's transformations is that each is established independently of other aspects of grammar, as Harris has emphasized. Each transformation is established once and for all from observation and evidence, on the basis of the distributional conditions I have just described; each transformational relation exists independently of what is true or false for the rest of the language. A transformation is in effect a generalization about the acceptability of instances of two sentence forms, and that factual generalization is true or false quite apart from anything we may subsequently discover about the language in question or the theory of language, or from any other source—say psychological experiment. This account is a natural one within the general approach of Harris's *Methods*—a nonpsychological conception of linguistics.

Harris rejects the idea that the language of a particular person or community can be regarded as a well-defined set of sentences with structures characterized by grammatical principles that are true or false. At least in the framework of his *Methods,* which provided the background for the development of the notion "transformation," a grammatical description is, as he put it, a compact account of a collection of data, and thus can be incorrect only through inadvertence—for example, if it states that some element in the data set has an observable property that it does not have. Transformational analysis, in his sense, is simply another way of describing the given collection of observations, and it is therefore quite natural to describe a transformation as a generalization stating that the data exhibit some property, in this case the property of equal acceptability under systematic substitution, as described a moment ago. A grammatical description in this sense is quite different from a (partial) theory in some natural science, for example. In the natural sciences, two theories may be in conflict even if they agree on available data, and the scientist will then search for new data to choose between them, proceeding on the "realist" assumption that what the theories allege about the entities postulated in them is true or false, and therefore susceptible to further test. But Harris, at least through the early sixties, took the position that alternative linguistic descriptions cannot be in conflict in this sense. At least, that is what I take him to be maintaining in work up to the time of his paper on transformational analysis in *Language.* [9]

In *LSLT* and subsequent work in generative grammar, transformations are defined in a very different manner. Perhaps I should have used a different term instead of adapting Harris's to the quite different context of generative grammar. In *LSLT,* for example, a transformation is not a relation between two sets of sentences or between two surface structures;* it is a rule within a system of rules that assigns structural descriptions to an infinite class of sentences. In the derivation of a particular sentence, a transformational rule applies to an abstract representation of this sentence and transforms it into another abstract representation. The initial representation is the so-called deep structure, which is transformed step by step into terminal (or surface) structure.

In the framework of generative grammar, equivalence relations of the kind that Harris uses to establish a transformation can only suggest the existence of a transformation, but not establish it. For example, in English it is true that the appropriate substitution relations between the active and the passive hold by and large: *Sincerity frightens Paul* is just as good a sentence as *Paul is frightened by sincerity,* while *Paul frightens sincerity* is just as bizarre as *Sincerity is frightened by Paul.* But no matter how precisely such substitution relations hold, they do not suffice to establish the existence of a transformation relating active and passive forms. Rather, empirical arguments are needed to show that within the schematism of permissible rule systems, the optimal grammar includes such a transformation. Furthermore, even if such a transformation is postulated on the basis of some empirical argument, it would not relate *Sincerity frightens Paul* and *Paul is frightened by sincerity.* Rather, the postulated passive transformation would figure in the derivation of *Paul is frightened by sincerity* from its abstract deep structure, but not in the derivation of *Sincerity frightens Paul* from its abstract deep structure; the two deep structures might be similar or even identical and the derivations identical apart from this transformation, but that is the only sense in

---

*The term *surface* must be understood as a technical one here. It does not signify that this structure cannot possess properties that are "intellectually profound." See below, p. 171.

which one might say that the two sentences are "related" by this transformation. Thus the notion "transformation" is quite different from the one that Harris developed.

Furthermore, within the theoretical framework of generative grammar a transformation is never "incorrigible" in Harris's sense. No matter how powerful the empirical evidence in favor of a grammar containing some transformation, subsequent evidence might indicate that the grammar is wrong and some other grammar permitted by the same general theory is right, or that the general theory is wrong and some different set of principles with a different schematism for grammar is right. Nor is it possible to determine, a priori, what kinds of evidence will prove relevant to such conclusions. A grammar is essentially like a hypothesis in the natural sciences concerning some subject matter—never finally established, no matter how strong the empirical evidence—and the same is true of a particular subhypothesis of the grammar to the effect that it contains a certain transformational rule.

I hope this helps to clarify the difference between the two conceptions.

Mathematics and Linguistics

M.R.:   Generative grammars were born of a meeting between mathematics and linguistics. Can you give more precise information about this birth?

N.C.:   I should distinguish between two questions. The first relates to a problem that has already been raised: How can linguistic knowledge be explicitly characterized? An explicit characterization must ultimately be a formalized theory. This remark may also be extended to the problem of acquisition of language and the related matter of explanatory theory, in the sense of our earlier discussion. Explanations exist to the degree that the general principles are precise—in principle, formalized; starting from such principles, one can construct a deductive argument leading to the phenomena that are to be explained.

Thus a certain quasi-mathematical mode of expression is presupposed in the overall program, but one that is quite unsophisticated. We want to formulate precise principles and precise rules within a formalized system. It turns out that the way to "speak precisely" is by formalization, but it would not be correct to consider that as mathematics. For example, some variety of recursive function theory provides the means, in principle, to express linguistic rules. But up to that point, this is formalization, not mathematics. Mathematical linguistics begins when one studies abstract properties of the formalization, abstracting away from particular realizations. The subject exists in a serious sense only insofar as nontrivial theorems can be proven, or at least considered. The viewpoint is very different.

M.R.:   Certain mathematical theories have seduced many linguists. I'm thinking of their "historic" encounters with telecommunications engineers . . .

N.C.:   Well, at the end of the forties and the beginning of the fifties, there were important developments in the mathematical theory of communication, information theory, and the theory of automata. Technically, models such as finite state Markov sources were proposed* . . .

Very often it was supposed that these models were appropriate for the description of language. Jakobson referred to this vaguely, but Hockett utilized them quite explicitly. In 1955 he proposed a theory of language structure based on a Markov source model borrowed from the mathematical theory of communication. Similar theories were developed by psychologists, engineers, mathematicians.

All these theories left me very skeptical. I became interested in the relevant mathematics at first largely because I wanted to

---

*Briefly, formal devices with a finite number of configurations (states) that produce sequences of symbols, one after the other, in a linear order, where the next symbol produced depends only on the present state and perhaps some input. In a linguistic application, the device might produce a sentence from left to right—first *The,* then *men,* then *arrived,* etc.—using the resources of a strictly finite memory to determine the next symbol.

prove that these models were not appropriate for the grammar of natural language.

M.R.: What was the a priori reason for your skepticism? An intuition?

N.C.: An intuition again founded on the same anti-empiricism. In my view, a finite state Markov source model might reasonably be considered as characterizing something like the outer limits of empiricist learning theory. In fact, a mathematical psychologist and logician, Patrick Suppes, gave precise expression to this intuition, or one version of it, a few years ago. He proved that a certain very rich version of stimulus-response learning theory must remain within the limits of finite state sources of the kind we have been discussing.

He considered this to be a positive result. To me it seemed to be a negative result. The reason is this. As has been known for a long time, even elementary systems of knowledge cannot be represented in terms of finite state Markov sources—for example, our knowledge of English, or even much simpler systems, such as propositional calculus. As a consequence, Suppes's result showed that knowledge which we possess cannot even be approached at the limit (a fortiori, not attained) by the learning theory he was considering. This constituted a final step in a complete refutation of this learning theory, and consequently, less powerful theories.

I did not believe in theories of language based on the Markov source model, which seemed to me to inherit the defects of empiricist learning theory. However, to know whether they were correct or not, it was necessary to wait until they were presented in a precise manner. Then the essential question could be posed:

Do properties of natural languages exist which cannot be expressed in any of these systems?

And such properties do exist.

M.R.: When did you demonstrate that?

N.C.: After *LSLT* was completed. The first version of this manuscript, completed in 1955, involved a good deal of formalization but no mathematics. Shortly after, I moved from the Society of Fellows at Harvard to the Research Laboratory of Electronics at MIT. There, there was a great deal of quite justified interest in the mathematical theory of communication, and also a great deal of—less justified—faith in the potential for the study of language offered by Markov source models and the like, which had aroused considerable enthusiasm among engineers, mathematical psychologists, and some linguists. As soon as the question was clearly formulated, it was immediately obvious that these models were not adequate for the representation of language. This observation was published in *Syntactic Structures,* and along with some other material, in a more technical article in 1956.

After that a certain branch of mathematical linguistics developed, which occupied itself primarily with the formal properties of systems that were considerably richer, called "phrase structure grammars." The most interesting class of these systems turned out to be what are called technically "context-free phrase structure grammars." Since the end of the fifties there has been quite a lot of work on the formal properties of various types of grammars, on their generative power, their properties and relations, and so on, and today this study constitutes a small branch of mathematics. The French mathematician M. P. Schützenberger made quite interesting contributions to this field . . .

M.R.: Which developed independently of linguistics . . .

N.C.: Yes, and I hope that these studies[10] will continue to be pursued, as well as the mathematical investigation of transformational grammars. There has been some interesting recent work by Stanley Peters and Robert Ritchie on this latter topic.

Returning to the earlier point, it seems clear that empiricist learning theories are much too limited to be adequate; and it is even possible to demonstrate this if we accept the assumption that finite state Markov sources are the richest systems that can be attained by such theories, at the limit. This conclusion does not seem to be unreasonable to me, although naturally it is not a precise conclusion because the notion "empiricist theory" is not well defined.

M.R.:   Did you link your critique of these theories right away to the critique of structural linguistics?

N.C.: Well, indirectly. These theories were then very much in fashion, and they even aroused a certain degree of euphoria, I think it is fair to say. In the intellectual milieu of Cambridge there was a great impact of the remarkable technological developments associated with World War II. Computers, electronics, acoustics, mathematical theory of communication, cybernetics, all the technological approaches to human behavior enjoyed an extraordinary vogue. The human sciences were being reconstructed on the basis of these concepts. It was all connected. As a student at Harvard in the early 1950s all of this had a great effect on me. Some people, myself included, were rather concerned about these developments, in part for political reasons, at least as far as my personal motivations were concerned.

M.R.:   For political reasons?

N.C.:   Yes, because this whole complex of ideas seemed linked to potentially quite dangerous political currents: manipulative, and connected with behaviorist concepts of human nature.

M.R.:   Thus your skepticism had political causes . . .

N.C.:   Yes, in part. But of course these motivations were irrelevant to showing that all this was wrong, as I thought it was. I believed that these theories could not really offer what they promised. As soon as they were analyzed carefully, they unraveled, though not without leaving substantive and important contributions.

M.R.:   We have seen vast programs of research on artificial intelligence develop, based on the apparently infinite capacities of computers . . .

N.C.   Artificial intelligence came a little later as an outgrowth of what was then called cybernetics . . .

M.R.:   The situation in this respect is paradoxical. In general, physics and technology permit the growth of human capacities and performance, sometimes with the aid of quite simple instruments. With artificial intelligence, the most advanced technology is developed to obtain the most limited results, well below the capacity of the most stupid creature . . .

N.C.:   I'm afraid that much of the work in this field relies on ideas that are too elementary and superficial to shed light on the question of human intelligence. This need not be the case, and perhaps some day will not be the case. But it has been true so far, by and large, and the field has also suffered from quite irresponsible claims. The same is true in the behavioral sciences, for example, Skinner's work on verbal behavior. That work, published in 1957, was presented ten years earlier as the William James Lectures. It immediately gained great influence. W. V. Quine, George Miller, and many others wrote and talked about it with considerable enthusiasm. It was quite the rage at about the time that I came to Cambridge, in 1951, at Harvard.

One could have thought—in fact, some people did think—that computers were going to permit the automation of discovery procedures in linguistics. The idea would be to present a corpus of material to the computer so that it would work out the grammar of this text, on the assumption that the taxonomic procedures of analysis that had been developed were in essence sufficient and adequate to determine grammatical structure. It was quite generally supposed, at least in the intellectual environment here in Cambridge, that the Skinnerian theory of behavior approached adequacy, and that the notions developed within the theory of communication, in particular the Markov source model, furnished a general framework for the study of language. But when I began to study these topics, I was quickly convinced that the prevailing assumptions were false and the popular models inadequate, for reasons which were not independent but had significant links, as I've already said, with empiricist dogma.

First Steps

M.R.:   What were your first contacts with the linguistic community? Hostile? Full of conflict?

N.C.:   Not exactly. In the beginning we ignored each other. For example, almost no one paid any attention to that first work I mentioned to you, on the generative grammar of Modern Hebrew. But that was the work of a student, and I did not expect that anyone would pay attention to it. As far as I know, only two linguists showed any interest in it: Henry Hoenigswald, an Indo-Europeanist with whom I studied at the University of Pennsylvania, and Bernard Bloch, the well-known Yale phonologist.

However, outside the field of linguistics proper the work attracted the attention of Yehoshua Bar-Hillel, who was then here in Cambridge—we became very close friends. He made some excellent suggestions. For example, he suggested very persuasively that I should be much more radical and should postulate much more abstract underlying representations, similar to those postulated for earlier stages of the language, to explain contemporary forms. That turned out to be a very good idea. The significance of his suggestion became apparent much later in generative phonology. I recast the Hebrew grammar completely, following this suggestion, in 1951, improving it considerably, I thought.

Quine expressed some interest in the methodological aspect, particularly the problem of constructing a simplicity measure for linguistic theory, and encouraged me to work further on that, as did Nelson Goodman. But that was about all. Among the linguists no one showed any interest in that type of work.

I wasn't particularly disturbed or surprised: I did not think myself that I was doing linguistics. In a sense I was completely schizophrenic at that time. I still thought that the approach of American structural linguistics was essentially right. As I told you, I spend a great deal of time trying to improve and to formalize discovery procedures, in order to overcome their obvious defects. But once they were made precise, they led manifestly to the wrong results. Still, for quite a long time I thought that the mistake was mine, due to wrong formulations. In 1953 I published an article in the *Journal of Symbolic Logic* in which I tried to develop a discovery procedure that I hoped might be the basis for something that would really work. That, for me, was real linguistics. What I was doing otherwise—attempting to construct an explanatory theory of generative grammar—seemed to me a different kind of work, on the side, so to speak.

Among my contemporaries there were a few who found that work interesting.

The only one who had always thought I should pursue this work and drop the whole discovery procedure business was Morris Halle. He was then a graduate student at Harvard, as I was too, and was also teaching at the same time at MIT. We met in 1951, became close friends, and had endless discussions. He thought that these discovery procedures did not make any sense. I don't remember his arguments, but I do remember disagreeing with him at that time. By 1953, I came to the same conclusion: if the discovery procedures did not work, it was not because I had failed to formulate them correctly but because the entire approach was wrong.

In retrospect I cannot understand why it took me so long to reach this conclusion—I remember exactly the moment when I finally felt convinced. On board ship in mid-Atlantic, aided by a bout of seasickness, on a rickety tub that was listing noticeably—it had been sunk by the Germans and now was making its first voyage after having been salvaged. It suddenly seemed that there was a good reason—the obvious reason—why several years of intense effort devoted to improving discovery procedures had come to naught, while the work I had been doing during the same period on generative grammars and explanatory theory, in almost complete isolation, seemed to be consistently yielding interesting results.

Once I had recognized that, progress was very rapid. In the next year and a half I wrote *LSLT,* which was about 1,000 typed pages, and almost all of what was contained in *Syntactic Structures* and the 1958 Texas Conference paper, and so on.

As for the reception accorded to *LSLT,* there is little to say. I've already told you that I did not have the impression the reaction on the part of linguists was surprising. I offered *LSLT* to the MIT Press—who refused it. Quite rightly, I think, because at that time the situation was very unfavorable for a general book on that subject, especially one by an unknown author. I also submitted a technical article on simplicity and explanation to the journal *Word,* at the suggestion of Roman Jakobson, but it was rejected virtually by return mail. So I had little hope of seeing any of this work published, at least in a linguistic journal. But frankly, that did not trouble me greatly. I had a research position at the Research Laboratory of Electronics at MIT, which I obtained thanks to Morris Halle and Roman Jakobson, and I taught Scientific French and Scientific German—though I was barely competent—and also some undergraduate linguistics, philosophy, and logic. I did not have any problem making a living, and was free to do the work that interested me.

I should emphasize that although there was very little interest in the work I was doing, at least among linguists, I had absolutely no cause for complaint as far as working conditions were concerned. On the contrary, I was extremely fortunate and knew it. Studying at Penn with Zellig Harris and Nelson Goodman was a highly stimulating experience, and I was very fortunate to be able to continue discussing the work I was doing with Harris, particularly while I was at Harvard from 1951 to 1955 at the Society of Fellows, where I had no responsibilities and was free to do as I wished with all the facilities of Harvard available, a remarkable opportunity. I spent a good deal of time in courses, seminars, discussions, primarily with philosophers at Harvard—Quine, Austin (who visited Harvard then), White, and others. It was a very lively and stimulating period in the Cambridge area for a student with my particular interests.

The research climate at MIT was close to ideal. I could not possibly have obtained a position in linguistics anywhere—I really was not professionally qualified by the standards of the field. At MIT there were no entrenched academic strongholds in the areas that interested me. Morris Halle and I and a few others were free to pursue our research, and later, to design a program of graduate studies. This absence of established structure, along with a general spirit of encouragement for innovation that seemed promising, made it possible for linguistics to flourish at MIT in way that for us at least would have been virtually out of the question elsewhere.

George Miller, who was then in the Harvard Psychology Department, also became interested, and we did some work together in the mid-fifties. He went on to develop an entirely new domain of psycholinguistics. With his help I was able to spend a rewarding year at the Institute for Advanced Study in Princeton in 1958–9. I should also mention my close friend Eric Lenneberg, who at that time was beginning his extremely interesting studies in the biology of language, working along rather similar lines.

Later on these topics began to gain some attention among linguists, at first at the Texas Conferences in 1958 and 1959, organized by Archibald Hill, to which I was invited. The discussions were animated and sharp, as you pointed out before. Unfortunately, the proceedings of the 1959 conference were never published. There I presented a paper on the generative phonology of English, in which I approached that subject very much in the manner of my work on Hebrew ten years before, but this time with much more confidence in the approach. In general, I published virtually nothing except in journals that were outside the field of linguistics in those years.

Questions of generative grammar attracted the attention of linguists primarily as a result of the publication of a thorough review by Robert Lees of *Syntactic Structures* in 1957 in *Language*. The monograph, which appeared in Holland, would not have been known, I imagine, had it not been for that review-article. Discussion moved to a more general forum in 1962 at the International Congress of Linguists, which was held that year at MIT. I gave a talk there which was later published as a monograph, in a revised form, *Current Issues in Linguistic Theory.* [11] In that talk I tried to explain, in a fairly comprehensive manner, what seemed to me to be the essential differences between generative grammar and structural linguistics. But it was still somewhat difficult to publish in the United States, although the situation had improved greatly with the publication of very important work by Robert Lees, G. H. Matthews, and Edward Klima.

M.R.: Did you now begin to teach linguistics?

N.C.: Yes, at the beginning of the sixties we began a program of graduate studies. As I mentioned, we were able to develop our program at MIT because, in a sense, MIT was outside the American university system. There were no large departments of humanities or the related social sciences at MIT. Consequently, we could build up a linguistics department without coming up against problems of rivalry and academic bureaucracy. Here we were really part of the Research Laboratory of Electronics. That permitted us to develop a program very different from any other and quite independent.

About the same time, a graduate program in psychology was established at MIT under Hans-Lukas Teuber's direction, and a little later a graduate program in philosophy was set up. Both developed in a way that was quite congenial to our work, and there has been a good deal of interaction among students and faculty, including joint appointments and jointly taught courses. That continues, and I expect that there will be even closer integration of these fields, along with related areas in engineering and computer science. It seems to me that there is a rather natural emerging discipline of cognitive psychology in which these various threads come together, and within which linguistics can find an appropriate place.

The First Students

M.R.: Who were the first students and the first researchers of that new program?

N.C.:   Morris Halle was already working on a generative phonology of Russian in the 1950s, and we also worked together on the generative phonology of English, at first jointly with Fred Lukoff. Together with Lees, Matthews, Klima, and Lukoff, I was, at least in principle, part of a research project on machine translation in the Research Laboratory of Electronics, headed by Victor Yngve. But the linguists, with the exception perhaps of Matthews, were not much interested in the applied problems of machine translation, as far as I can remember. At the end of the fifties, Matthews, who was a specialist in American Indian languages and had a good mathematical background as well, produced a very important grammar of Hidatsa.

In the technical sense of the term, Robert Lees was our first student, though in reality a colleague. He presented his Ph.D. thesis, on English nominalizations, in 1960. But actually he received an engineering degree. Klima, who worked with us, received his Ph.D. degree at Harvard on historical syntax. He also published a very important and influential article on negation. When the graduate program began, Jerry Fodor and Jerry Katz were here, as was Paul Postal. John Viertel, who was also on the machine translation program, was beginning his work on Humboldt and related topics at that time, and M.-P. Schützenberger was visiting from France. After that, things went very fast . . .

M.R.:   That was the birth of the Standard Theory . . .

N.C.:   Yes, it was at that period that what was called the Standard Theory was formulated, with major contributions by Fodor, Katz, and Postal, and many students in the new graduate program, a large number of whom are now among the most productive scholars in the field, which has really changed quite dramatically since the period we have just been discussing.

CHAPTER 6

Semantics

I have said above that Chomsky's first model—the model of Syntactic Structures—*contained essentially three components: the rewriting rules, the transformational rules, and the morphophonological rules. In 1965 a significantly different model appeared. The tradition that begins with* Aspects of the Theory of Syntax *(1965) presents this model in the following manner. The* base component *consists of two elements: the rewriting rules which, as before, indicate the structure of sequences of words; and the lexicon, to which are assigned all the syntactic, semantic, and phonological properties of the lexical items. The base grammar generates the initial phrase marker, or the* deep structure.

The transformational component *transforms this initial structure into other structures, the last of which is termed the* surface structure. *The base component and the transformational component constitute the generative part of the model.*

One of the most important innovations of Aspects *is the introduction of two* interpretive components, *the phonological component and the semantic component. Here the status of the morphophonology has in some way changed. But the semantic component, at least in the form that was integrated into Chomsky's model at the suggestion of Fodor, Katz, and Postal, was something completely new. Fodor, Katz, and Postal sought to extend the concept of generative grammar to the domain of meaning. Chomsky wanted to make explicit what the speaker knows of syntactic structure. In the same way, they wanted to make explicit what the speaker knows of the "intrinsic" meaning of words and sentences. Toward that end they proposed a model consisting of two parts: in the one part, each word was assigned a description of the following type: X is + or – animate; + or – female; + or – solid; + or – transparent; etc.—this is part of the lexicon. In the other part, rules called "projection rules" compared the properties of words to indicate whether their combination within a sentence was acceptable or not.*

The semantic component was to be integrated with the generative grammar at the level of deep structure: it is this syntactic structure which receives the meaning. The Standard Theory is generally visualized in terms of the following schema:

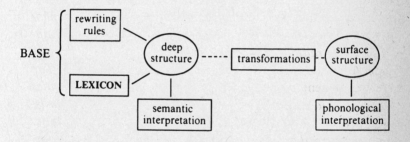

But this model was soon challenged, in particular, as we shall see, because of the exclusive link it postulated between semantics and deep structure.

The Role of Semantics in Grammar

M.R.:   With the Standard Theory we enter into the second period in the history of generative grammar, the period in which semantics became the center of discussion.

N.C.:   Yes, but it should not be forgotten that the theory which preceded this did explicitly presuppose a general semantic theory, based in part on the work of Goodman and Quine, and in part on Wittgenstein and the Oxford school. I'm speaking now of *LSLT* and *Syntactic Structures.* Contrary to what has been said—there has been a great deal of misunderstanding on this subject—this work accorded a central place to semantics. However, I was skeptical about the general belief that syntax was based on semantic considerations, which is quite a different matter. Many structural linguists and many philosophers—Quine, for example—claimed that grammatical concepts must be defined on the basis of semantic notions. For example, that the concept of phoneme must be defined in terms of synonymy . . .

M.R.:   Which means saying that *r* and *l* are different phonemes because *ramp* and *lamp* don't have the same meaning . . .

N.C.:   Yes, that's one example. Or they also identified the concept of grammaticality with the notion of meaningfulness. But it seemed to me that a grammatical sentence may not have any literal meaning . . .

M.R.:   That was behind the discussion about the sentence which became quite famous, *Colorless green ideas sleep furiously.* For you, this is grammatical, even if it does not rank highest in the degree of grammaticalness. Accordingly, you require that grammatical concepts be defined in terms that are formal and specific, independent of vague semantic notions.

N.C.:   Furthermore, I tried to show that every clear formulation of a hypothesis concerning the alleged necessity to define syntactic notions in semantic terms led to incorrect results. Thinking about these questions led to what was later termed the hypothesis of *autonomy of syntax.*

The more I think about it, the more it seems to me that this thesis is quite natural . . . I also know of no substantive argument that it is incorrect. In the context of language acquisition, the hypothesis implies that one learns the meaning of an expression with a form established on independent grounds. One cannot "pick up" a disembodied meaning that floats about in the air and then construct a form which expresses it. It isn't easy to make much sense of any of this. It seems to me that the elements of syntax are not established on a semantic basis, and that the mechanisms of syntax, once they have been constructed, function independently of the other components of the grammar, which are interpretive components.

M.R.: This hypothesis also explains why speakers arrive at similar phonological and syntactic systems, while the meaning given to words by their experiences may be very different.

N.C.: I think, in fact, that the thesis of the autonomy of syntax, in the form proposed in the fifties and since then, is probably correct. However, I have always explicitly denied and rejected a totally different position which has often been attributed to me: namely, that the study of meaning and reference and of the use of language should be excluded from the field of linguistics. What I said was exactly the opposite. A large part of *Syntactic Structures* and *LSLT* is devoted to the problem of semantic interpretation of formal systems. In fact, these questions were central in both *Syntactic Structures* and *LSLT.* I tried to show that some interesting and moderately subtle aspects of semantic interpretation of sentences can be explained in part in terms of a theory of linguistic levels, developed within the framework of generative transformational grammar. I also argued explicitly that semantic considerations enter in an essential manner into the choice of a correct linguistic theory. Thus the viewpoint of this work was that, given a linguistic theory, the concepts of grammar are constructed (so it seems) on the basis of primitive notions that are not semantic (where the grammar contains the phonology and syntax), but that the linguistic theory itself must be chosen so as to provide the best possible explanation of semantic phenomena, as well as others. Apparently many linguists have failed to make this distinction, and have concluded that I intended to exclude consideration of semantics, when the exact opposite is true: I argued explicitly that semantic considerations are essential for linguistic theory, as I have just said, and devoted a large part of these two books to the defense of that position.

In terms of our preceding discussion, linguistic theory (or "universal grammar") is what we may suppose to be biologically given, a genetically determined property of the species: the child does not learn this theory, but rather applies it in developing knowledge of language. It would be absurd to suppose that this innate linguistic theory, which determines the general form and structure of language, should not be connected in the most intimate manner to the fundamental properties of meaning and language use. Moreover no one, to my knowledge, has ever proposed such an absurd idea, though there has been a great deal of confusion about this subject in the literature.

M.R.:   In my opinion, the misunderstanding derives from the fact that the word *semantics* embraces a number of different definitions, and that yours does not correspond to theirs. They remain bound to the definition that is inherent in the traditional logic-derived grammars, which make grammatical concepts dependent on semantic notions. Think of their formulas: *The subject carries out the action, The object suffers the action,* and so on. If you take this semantics away from them, nothing remains. And if, according to them, semantics does not play this primary role, then it does not play any role at all.

N.C.:   It seems that two questions are confused: one is the question of the autonomy of syntax; the other is whether the study of meaning and reference belongs to the study of language. There isn't really any problem about that. Everyone has always taken for granted that a central concern of generative grammar is to incorporate linguistic semantics.

The "Fodor-Katz" Hypothesis

M.R.:   Very quickly, among those who have accepted the autonomy of syntax, two tendencies can be discerned. Some make the semantic component a representation of the world, while others limit it to very precise and testable problems . . .

N.C.:   Personally, in my earliest work *(Syntactic Structures* and *LSLT)* I had in mind a dual theory of meaning, in some sense. On the one hand, I referred to Goodman's attempt to extend the theory of reference to some parts of the theory of meaning, and also to Quine's influential, and I think rather persuasive, critique of a number of standard approaches to the theory of meaning. On the other hand, I had in mind the Oxford theories of language use.

When Fodor and Katz proposed integrating in the Standard Theory rules of semantic interpretation which associated semantic *representations* with syntactic structures, they had in mind something entirely different from what I had proposed. The Standard Theory incorporated their proposals as an innovation. Their rules had an *intensional* character, which did not exist in *Syntactic Structures,* where no linguistic level of *semantic representation* was envisaged. They developed an analogy between phonetics and semantics. Just as the phonetic representation is based on a universal system of phonetic features, so the semantic representation would be based on a universal system of semantic categories, or semantic "distinctive features." The universal system is supposed to be able to represent all possible conceptual thought. Katz takes the view that a semantic theory in his sense should aim to give a complete characterization of the semantic properties of all utterances of all languages, independent of all extralinguistic considerations—an account of whatever can be expressed in any language, whatever can be thought.

It is not at all clear that there exists such a universal semantic system. Perhaps there are semantic properties that are general, universal, of the type proposed by Katz and others. It seems reasonable to suppose that at least traditional notions like "agent of action," "instrument," "goal," "source," and so on, are part of universal semantics; then such notions would be available for semantic representation, perhaps in the sense in which phonological features are available for phonological representation. Julius Moravcsik has discussed the Aristotelian origins of several of these fundamental notions in some very interesting recent work. Furthermore, there seem to be more specific properties which enter into the analysis of the verbal system, for example. To take a case that has been frequently discussed, it seems reasonable to suppose that semantic relations between words like *persuade, intend, believe,* can be expressed in purely linguistic terms (namely: If I persuade you to go, then you intend to go; If I persuade you that today is Tuesday, then you believe that today is Tuesday. These are facts of language and not of the external world). Furthermore, it also seems reasonable to suppose that the fundamental properties of quantifiers (words like *all, any, some,* etc.) and anaphora (the relations between antecedents and pronouns, for example) can be expressed in part on the level of semantic representation, separate from extralinguistic considerations. If so, then these aspects of the theory of meaning can be taken to fall within the "generative grammar," understood as the system of rules that specifies our purely linguistic knowledge of the sound and the meaning of sentences. I might add that apparently divergent approaches tend to be in fairly close agreement, apart from their terminology, about such conclusions.

Why, then, raise a question about the possibility of a universal semantics, which would provide an exact representation of the full meaning of each lexical item, and the meaning of expressions in which these items appear? There are, I believe, good reasons for being skeptical about such a program. It seems that other cognitive systems—in particular, our system of beliefs concerning things in the world and their behavior—play an essential part in our judgments of meaning and reference, in an extremely intricate manner, and it is not at all clear that much will remain if we try to separate the purely linguistic components of what in informal usage or even in technical discussion we call "the meaning of linguistic expression." I doubt that one can separate semantic representation from beliefs and knowledge about the world.

To be sure, someone who believes in a level of representation of the type proposed by Katz can reply: "In doing so, I propose a *legitimate idealization.* I assume, with Frege, that there exist semantic elements common to all languages, independent of everything except language and thought. In rejecting this idealization, you make the same mistake as those who confuse pragmatics with syntax."

Certainly, this objection has some force. But I doubt that it will wholly withstand further reflection. Whenever concepts are examined with care, it seems that they involve beliefs about the real world. This idea is not new: Wittgenstein and Quine, among others, have emphasized that our use of concepts is set within a system of beliefs about lawful behavior of objects; similar ideas have been attributed to Leibniz. Thus, when we use the terms *chair* or *table*, we rely on beliefs concerning the objects to which we refer. We assume that they will not disappear suddenly, that they will fall when they are let go, and so on. These assumptions are not part of the meaning of *chair*, etc., but if the assumptions fail we might conclude that we were not referring to a chair, as we had thought.

In studying semantics one must keep in mind the role of nonlinguistic systems of belief: we have our expectations about three dimensional space, about texture and sensation, about human behavior, inanimate objects, and so on. There are many mental organs in interaction.

To repeat an observation of Wittgenstein's, we would not know how to name an object if at one moment it looked like a chair, and a moment later disappeared, that is to say, if it does not obey the laws of nature. The question: "Is that a chair or not?" would not have an answer according to strictly linguistic criteria. Admittedly it is difficult to establish such conclusions. Too little is understood about cognitive *systems* and their interaction. Still, this approach seems reasonable to me; to give it some real content, it would be necessary to discover something comparable to a generative grammar in the domain of factual knowledge, which is no small task. My own speculation is that only a bare framework of semantic properties, altogether insufficient for characterizing what is ordinarily called "the meaning of a linguistic expression," can be associated correctly with the idealization "language."

The Truth of Sentences

M.R.:   In Katz's semantic component, there is not only the universal semantics, independent of knowledge of the world, but also the *projection rules,* whose role is to exclude sentences devoid of meaning. This mechanism would exclude *Colorless green ideas sleep furiously,* because it cannot be true that ideas are green, and one cannot sleep furiously . . . But does that not mean reintroducing a notion—the "truth" of propositions—which has nothing to do with grammar?

N.C.:   Everybody believes that truth conditions are some-how related to semantic representation. However, the question is far from simple. On this subject, John Austin has given some interesting examples. Take the sentence: *New York is 200 miles from Boston.* Is it true or false? If the statement is made in answer to a question that you ask in order to find out how long it will take you to go by car, four hours or four days, it is true. But if you have just 10 gallons of gas, and I know that your car will do 20 miles per gallon, and you want to know whether you can go from Boston to New York without stopping, then the statement is false if the real distance is 210 miles. And so on.

Thus all sorts of considerations determine the truth conditions of a statement, and these go well beyond the scope of grammar.

Suppose I say: *The temperature is falling.* Nobody knows exactly what that means without extralinguistic presuppositions. Does it mean that the temperature is lower than it was five minutes ago? Perhaps. But if I say: *The temperature is falling,* meaning that we are heading toward an ice age, then my statement may be true even if the temperature is rising locally. Even for the simplest sentences it is impossible to set truth conditions, outside the context of language use. And we must also distinguish fixed beliefs, temporary beliefs, etc.

M.R.:   Can one summarize what you have said by contrasting two conceptions of semantics: the one, "extensional," presented in *Syntactic Structures,* treated the relation between certain elements of language and external objects (for example, anaphora): the other, "intensional," which claims, as Katz does, to account for all meanings of words and sentences without appealing to our knowledge of the world? In this respect, the work of Ray Jackendoff[1] belongs to the conception of *Syntactic Structures*.

N.C.: I'm not quite in agreement with that characterization. Thus I agree with Katz that certain analytic connections exist among linguistic expressions, certain truths hold solely by virtue of linguistic facts: for instance, the relation between *I persuaded him to leave* and *He intends to leave,* which I mentioned a little while ago. In such cases we are dealing with properties of semantic representation that are "intensional" and are strictly part of "grammar," in a natural sense of the term. The same is true of the so-called thematic relations ("agent," "goal," etc.) developed in a very interesting manner in the work of Jackendoff which you have mentioned. One might say that this work of Jackendoff's is quite compatible with the program of *Syntactic Structures,* but he developed a semantic theory in a direction that was not in any fashion proposed or suggested there.

M.R.: This is what is called "interpretive semantics" ... Recently you have replaced *semantic representation* by the expression *logical form.* Can you explain the nature of this change?

N.C.: I used the expression *logical form* really in a manner different from its standard sense, in order to contrast it with *semantic representation.* I used the expression *logical form* to designate a level of linguistic representation incorporating all semantic properties that are strictly determined by linguistic rules. To determine the precise relation between "logical form," so defined, and semantic theory and description, which inextricably involves contributions from other cognitive systems—that stands as an important question. Recent work has some interesting suggestions on this matter.

M.R.:   As far as co-reference is concerned—that is, the question of the relation between nouns and pronouns and extralinguistic objects—certain laws are linguistic, others belong to discourse.

N.C.:   In the case of co-reference, the matter is reasonably well understood. There exist principles that are completely linguistic. For example, in *John sees him, John* and *him* cannot be taken to refer to the same person, that is to say, they cannot be co-referential (though to be precise, it is intended rather than actual co-reference that is at issue). That is a linguistic rule. Similarly, in *John expected him to leave, John* and *him* cannot be co-referential. Take a more complex case: *I seem to John to like him.* Here *John* and *him* can be co-referential, but in *John seems to me to like him, John* and *him* cannot be co-referential. In this case it seems that we are dealing with rules of sentence grammar, which satisfy the general conditions that govern such rules.

M.R.:   In French we find an almost identical difference in *Marie regarde Pierre le coiffer,* where *Pierre* and *le* cannot be co-referential, while in *Pierre regarde Marie le coiffer, Pierre* and *le* can be co-referential.

N.C.:   In all these cases there is a network of relations that determines what can be and what cannot be co-referential, and these relations are governed by principles that form part of the grammar. For example, the difference between *Pierre believes he is intelligent* and *He believes Pierre is intelligent* is due to what are called relations of "command": co-reference is impossible if the pronoun is located "higher" in the phrase structure than its nonpronominal antecedent. Now in the second case *Pierre* is found in a subordinated position, thus "lower" than *he,* so that they cannot be co-referential in the relevant sense.

M.R.:   In the majority of cases, English and French present analogous facts. In other, more subtle cases they differ. For example, in English one can say: *Harry thought it was impossible to wash himself in such conditions,* where *himself* refers back to *Harry.* In French a word-for-word translation of this sentence would be bizarre. It is necessary to add a pronoun in the subordinate clause: *Henri pensa qu'il LUI était impossible de se laver (lui-même) dans telles conditions.*

N.C.: Why is this so? These are interesting questions. One does not know what these phenomena indicate until one finds the rules that explain them. All this belongs to the first category of anaphoric relations.

In the second category we have the problem of determining the reference of words such as *the others* or even *he* in sentences of the type: *He has arrived, Some reacted well, but the others were angry* . . . It is not grammatical principles (or more precisely, principles of sentence grammar) which govern the relations of these pronouns to their antecedents or intended referents. There are many other conventions in discourse beyond the rules of sentence grammar. If I say, while showing you this photograph, *He is a good kid,* that would be quite correct, because it is perfectly acceptable to present this boy to you in this way in this context: we are looking at a photograph on my desk, and we share certain assumptions about photographs, and specifically photographs that one puts on one's desk; you imagine that this is a photograph of my son because otherwise it wouldn't be there, and so on. Thus, in a much larger context which is not linguistic but rich in beliefs of varied sorts, my statement is perfectly appropriate. But these conventions of reference are not part of grammar. To express them would require a richer theory, integrating a number of cognitive systems, including your assumptions about what one expects to see on my desk. All that plays a role in what some might call the full semantic representation.

To develop the inferences that follow from this statement, we would have to consider the "reference" of pictures and all the assumptions concerning the persons about whom I am likely to talk, their relations to me, etc. The actual reference of linguistic expressions in real life involves the interaction of cognitive systems. And grammar is only one of these. Much the same is true of most of our concepts, which are embedded within systems of belief about the nature of the world; the latter enter into the kind of semantic representation required to account for legitimate reference, truth conditions, speech acts, and so on.

Interpretive Semantics and Generative Semantics

M.R.:   We have just seen that Katz's semantic component, which he formulated in 1963, with its reference to a universal semantic system, has been challenged. However, it is what gave birth, toward the end of the sixties, to a "schismatic" tendency, which is opposed to generative grammar in its "Standard" form: generative semantics. Due to a further misunderstanding, this generative semantics has also been attributed to you. Briefly summarized, this theory rejects the autonomy of syntax with respect to semantics, and claims that the deep structure is to be identified with the semantic representation.

Today generative semantics in its initial form has been virtually abandoned (to the degree that there is no new formulation to replace it by improving it), although all kinds of people doing all kinds of things doubtless continue to call themselves "generative semanticists." In the beginning its principal proponents were Postal, McCawley, Ross, Lakoff . . . also Fillmore.

It was a vogue that still endures in certain European countries like Germany and France.

It seems to me that these theories have recapitulated the weaknesses for which you criticized structuralism, in abandoning the goals of linguistics which you formulated: to explain the acquisition of language. They forget that they were dealing with something real . . .

N.C.:   My feeling is that this work tended to return to a kind of descriptivism. In the case of Fillmore, this is quite explicit. In an article entitled, I believe, "The New Taxonomy," he describes himself as a taxonomist, a descriptivist, and quite rightly. If that is what interests him, I certainly have no criticism; furthermore, he is doing very good work in descriptive semantics. Once again, there's just no argument that one can

have about this issue, just as there can't be any argument between someone who does natural history and someone who is
looking for biological principles. These are different occupa-
tions. Presumably they can learn something from one another.

For the moment Fillmore is not trying to construct a general
semantic theory; he does not want to base his work on any
comprehensive and explicit theory of language, if I understand
him correctly. Rather, he is producing material of greater or
lesser interest, which a semantic theory may be able to use some
day.

As for "generative semantics," it is difficult to discuss it
because nobody, to my knowledge, now advocates an explicit
theoretical position under that name. It is now nothing but a
rather loose characterization covering the work of a number of
people. Insofar as a theory had been clearly formulated, it
seems to have generally been abandoned—at least as far as I
know—by those who formulated it. Postal is doing quite different things today. I don't know what he currently thinks about
generative semantics, but in any case, his recent work—relational grammar—seems to me quite remote from it. In fact, he
seems to have put aside the question of the relations between
meaning and form, if I understand his most recent work correctly, but perhaps I do not.

John Ross, another important figure in that movement, is
working on what he calls non-discrete grammar, that is to say,
a theory based on graded concepts rather than discrete categories.

M.R.:   That is the theory of "squish," where a word is not
defined by its category, but is "a bit of a noun, a lot of a verb,
and just a little bit of adjective" . . .

N.C.:   And so on. He is also interested in the interaction of
pragmatics, syntax, and semantics. Therefore, not in generative
semantics, at least in the earlier sense of this term. Furthermore, I believe he considers it premature or even wrong to seek
an explicit theory.

Lakoff is doing similar work. He is working on "cognitive grammar," which integrates language with nonlinguistic systems. I don't see any theory in prospect there.

In general, I remain skeptical about these latter approaches. They do not distinguish things that seem to me easily distinguishable, for example, grammatical competence from other factors that enter into linguistic behavior. That creates confusion. As for the rest, there is nothing to discuss, because there is now no substantive theory under the heading of "generative semantics."

Where then does the expression "generative semantics" come from? It is a general attitude or point of view which was expressed, for example, by Lakoff in an article entitled "Generative Semantics," or by Postal in his 1969 article "The Best Theory." But nobody—at least not to my knowledge—has accepted this theory, which in the form presented was virtually empty. What the theory asserted was that there exist representations of meaning, representations of form, and relations between the two. Furthermore, these relations between the two representations were virtually arbitrary; Lakoff, in the paper I just cited, proposed arbitrary derivational constraints*—arbitrary rules in effect. If all that is put forward as a theory is that there exist relations between some kind of representation of meaning and of form, then it is difficult to argue about that.

As you said, what was happening in these years has often been misinterpreted. In fact, the Standard Theory, as presented in *Aspects,* for example, was questioned from the very beginning. On the one hand, it was noted in the book itself (which went to press in 1964), that at least some aspects of semantic representation, for example those related to topic and comment, seem to involve surface structure rather than deep struc-

---

*These are constraints on the application of grammatical rules. In the Standard Theory these restrictions apply uniquely to the transition from one structure in a derivation to the next. For Lakoff they apply to any structure at all, which makes them arbitrary and ad hoc. See G. Lakoff, "On Generative Semantics," in D. Steinberg and L. Jacobovits, eds., *Semantics: An Interdisciplinary Reader* (Cambridge, Mass.: MIT Press, 1971).

ture. Subsequent research on the role of surface structure in determining the meaning of a sentence led to what has been called the Extended Standard Theory. On the other hand, in *Aspects* I indicated that there were very different possibilities, for example, some work by Thomas Bever and Peter Rosenbaum, in which a virtual obliteration of the distinction between syntactic and semantic rules was proposed, an idea that led finally to generative semantics. The class of theories that can be developed as alternatives to the theory presented in *Aspects* is vast, and it is indicated there that it would be premature to exclude them with any conviction. The first person who offered a substantial critique of the Standard Theory, and the best, as far as I can recall, was Ray Jackendoff—that must have been in 1964 or 1965. He showed that surface structure played a much more important role in semantic interpretation than had been supposed; if so, then the Standard hypothesis, according to which it was the deep structure that completely determined this interpretation, is false. For example, by studying the interaction of negation and quantification within a sentence, Jackendoff showed that their relative position in the surface structure of the sentence was crucial for interpretation.* Many other such examples were worked out by Ray Dougherty and others.

These observations naturally were of great interest to me. They led a number of linguists to develop what came to be called the Extended Standard Theory. But at the same time that

---

* *Many arrows didn't hit the target, but many did hit it. Not many arrows hit the target, but many have hit it. Not many demonstrators were arrested by the police. Many of the demonstrators were not arrested by the police.*

Another well-known example of a change of meaning depending on the position of quantifiers in the surface structure is presented by the passive-active dichotomy:

Many people are buying the same brands of cigarettes.

The same brands of cigarettes are bought by many people.

The first case can be interpreted as saying that people are faithful to their brand; the second that certain brands are more successful.

Similar but less convincing examples were already noted in *Syntactic Structures* and *LSLT,* even then indicating the role of surface structure in semantic interpretation. But Jackendoff was the first to account for these phenomena in a systematic manner, and thus to integrate them in the theory by proposing interpretive rules.

the Standard Theory was modified to accommodate the role of surface structure, others took a contrary path, relying on a different intuition: they drew the connection between semantic representation and deep structure more closely, to the point where the two became identical. That is of course generative semantics. So described, the basic position is incorrect, because the hypothesis shared with the Standard Theory is false, as I've just pointed out.

Accordingly, to incorporate the role of surface structure in determining semantic representation without abandoning the identification of deep structure and semantic representation, generative semantics introduced the notion of "global rules," that is, rules that relate noncontiguous steps in a derivation; specifically, that relate the underlying abstract semantic representation and those properties of surface structure that enter into the determination of meaning.

Note that these global rules that relate surface structure to the semantic representation, postulated by generative semantics, are quite similar, if not identical, to the interpretive rules proposed by Jackendoff and others. It was quickly proposed that global rules may appear quite generally in the grammar, in phonology as well as in syntax and semantics. A theory that permits global rules has immense descriptive potential. As I've said, to approach an "explanatory" linguistic theory, or— which is the same thing—to account for the possibility of language acquisition, it is necessary to reduce severely the class of accessible grammars. Postulating global rules has just the opposite effect, and therefore constitutes a highly undesirable move, which must be supported by substantial arguments. I do not believe that such arguments have been presented. On the contrary, it does not appear to me that any convincing evidence have been produced in support of global rules.

The situation grew even worse—if that is possible—when generative semanticists began to incorporate nonlinguistic factors into grammar: beliefs, attitudes, etc. That amounts to a rejection of the initial idealization to language, as an object of study. A priori, such a move cannot be ruled out, but it must be empirically motivated. If it proves to be correct, I would conclude that language is a chaos that is not worth studying— but personally I do not believe that any evidence or substantive arguments have been brought forward in favor of such a hypothesis. Note that the question is not whether belief or attitudes, and so on, play a role in linguistic behavior or linguistic judgments. Of course they do, no one has ever doubted that. The question is whether distinct cognitive structures can be identified, which interact in the real use of language and linguistic judgments, the grammatical system being one of these.

Certainly, in the real world everything enters into interaction. But if a physicist had to consider motion pictures of people walking down the street, he would abandon all hope of doing physics. We come back to the question of rationality and idealization.

The people who are working on non-discrete grammars, or on what remains of generative semantics, have not given any substantial reason, as far as I know, for objecting to standard idealizations. It is possible that these idealizations will create problems, and will prove ultimately to be incorrect, in detail or perhaps even in principle. I mentioned some possible examples when we were discussing semantic representation. But I do not have the impression that any significant objection has been presented in the work in generative semantics, on "non-discrete" or "cognitive" grammars. On the contrary, it seems to me that people working in these directions are allowing themselves to be submerged by the phenomena.

M.R.: In the same way, have they not been diverted from what you consider the real goal of linguistics: explaining the acquisition of language?

N.C.: They would not agree, I suppose, but I believe it is true. Nevertheless, we are talking about a straw man: generative semantics does not now exist, in any reasonably well-defined sense of the term. The term *generative semantics* remains, but today its content has become completely obscure.

M.R.: Still, its brief success seemed brilliant, and I began to ask myself at that time whether the reason for that was not ideological, as in the case of empiricism. It was a way of going back to the dominant structuralism. Often the intellectuals have thought that they could avoid the issue of generative grammar by leaping over a stage: directly from structuralism to Lakoff's semantics . . .

N.C.: Perhaps. They are in fact rather similar. A number of linguists, particularly you yourself in your article on "Remind," as well as Ray Dougherty and Bever and Katz and some others, have tried to establish a connection between generative semantics and neo-Bloomfieldian descriptivism, quite persuasively, in my opinion.

M.R.: The case grammars of Fillmore have had a great deal of success in France as a result of the translation of one of his articles in the journal *Langages*.

N.C.: Here again it seems to me that there is a great deal of misunderstanding about what is going on. Case grammar is based on certain assumptions that are common to all linguistic theory, namely, that between verbs and noun phrases there are such relations as "agent," "instrument," "goal," and so on. Take the Standard Theory, in the form presented, say, by Jerrold Katz. It incorporates a system of "semantic relations" that are very difficult to distinguish from the "cases" of Fillmore, that is, if they are not completely indistinguishable.

Take the Extended Standard Theory: it incorporates thematic relations of the sort studied by Jackendoff, expanding on earlier work by J. Gruber. Every semantic description includes something like a "case grammar," at least insofar as this theory simply proposes that the familiar semantic relations, which are also discussed in the traditional grammars, link verbs to noun phrases. The interesting question is how to integrate this "case grammar" into the theory of language . . .

M.R.: And not to substitute case grammar for the theory of language . . .

N.C.: Yes, the question of integration remains open; one can disagree about it. In my opinion, quite solid empirical arguments have been advanced against the particular theses of Fillmore's case grammars. In particular, such arguments have been presented by Ray Dougherty and several others, myself included. I do not know what Fillmore thinks about this at present. As I've said, right now he seems to be more interested in descriptive semantics—his "new taxonomy"—than in problems of general linguistic theory, if I understand him correctly. But if one thinks of "case grammar" as nothing other than the theory which incorporates the traditional semantic relations in a certain form, without any more specific hypotheses as to their nature or their integration within generative grammar, then we have a system with which one can work easily, at least in a superficial way. It is sufficient to take any language and to designate in each sentence the agent, the instrument, the goal, etc., and one will have a case grammar in this restricted sense, which is without much interest. That isn't even applied linguistics. Let me emphasize again: this is not Fillmore's "case grammar," which did put forth specific hypotheses, but ones that were, I believe, shown to be incorrect.

M.R.: That is curious, this repugnance for studying syntactic structures.

N.C.: I would say the same about the study of semantic structures. Because any nontrivial research in semantics must go much further than these elementary concepts. Think of phonology: if a phonological theory merely says: "There are vowels and there are consonants," then it isn't a very interesting theory, because all theories are in accord on this point, no matter what differences there may be otherwise. The question becomes interesting when we ask: "How is the category 'vowel' integrated in a serious theory of phonological structure?"

It is the same thing in semantics. It is very important to discover how the categories recognized by everyone (under their different names) are to be integrated into a general theory, and to refine and elaborate these categories. If not, you are just doing taxonomy. In this respect I should mention some recent work by Jackendoff, which moves toward an "explanatory" semantics in quite an interesting way, integrating the "thematic relations" (or "cases") in a more general theory. That seems to be very promising work.

M.R.:   You have mentioned the new "relational grammar" of Postal. This is a grammar which, it is said, formulates its rules in terms of *functions* and not, as generative grammar proposes, in terms of syntactic categories. For example, the passive is expressed by saying: "An object becomes a subject." Generative grammar says: "Such a noun phrase, occurring within the structure *X,* can be placed within the structure *Y.* " Generative grammar presents arguments for not employing functions in the formulation of transformations. Postal seems to be proposing a return to Jespersen in order to reinforce his position.

N.C.:   Before talking about relational grammar and the passive, I want to say a few words about Jespersen. On the one hand, Jespersen was writing more or less as a philosopher, for example, in his *Philosophy of Grammar;* on the other hand as a grammarian, in his work on English grammar. In his philosophical work he is one of the first in this century to have stressed the notion of "free expression," what I have called the "creative" aspect of language. Here he went a good deal further than the structuralists, including Saussure, who had only quite primitive things to say on this subject. It is only due to the tools furnished by modern logic that this notion, discussed in some form by Descartes and Humboldt, for example, can now be studied seriously. Moreover, Jespersen devoted a large part of his *Philosophy of Grammar* to what has more recently been called "the autonomy of syntax." He raised the question of the relation between "notional concepts" and those of formal grammar, and had some quite interesting things to say about this. All that brings him close to contemporary concerns. I've written about this in a paper called "Questions of Form and Interpretation," given at the fiftieth anniversary of the Linguistic Society of America.

The situation is more complex when one turns to his work as a grammarian. Although he introduced a certain number of interesting innovations, I think it is fair to say that for the most part he remained within the framework of traditional grammar which, as I've already pointed out, offers examples and descriptions without giving the explicit principles that account for them. He did not formulate the problem of designing an explicit linguistic theory. But his work remains a mine of perceptive and useful observations and insights.

Now what is the connection between Jespersen and "relational grammar"? In the first place, it is difficult to discuss this precisely, because up to now (January 1976) this grammatical theory has not been presented in a systematic manner. It remains to be seen just exactly how it is related to various other approaches.

Certainly Jespersen, like all traditional grammarians, relies very heavily on the concept of grammatical relation. But what does that concept involve? It is not very clear. The term is used in many ways. For example, there is the notion of "thematic relations"—or the "cases" of "case grammar." One may say that in the two sentences: *The key opens the door* and *John opens the door with the key,* the noun phrase *The key* and the verb *open* enter into the same type of "thematic relation," namely, "instrument." Here we have one notion of grammatical relation—a semantic notion.

There is also a purely formal notion. Take for example the sentence: *I promised John that I would leave.* Formally we have a direct object, because no preposition separates the verb from its complement; but in another sense, this is an indirect object, a dative. The French translation of that sentence, *J'ai promis à Jean de partir,* contains a formal indirect object, as does the nominalized form in English: *My promise to John to leave.* For that sentence one must therefore distinguish two notions of "grammatical relations." Furthermore, insofar as one might also argue that *John* is the goal of the action, according to the thematic relations, there are three different things to distinguish. Perhaps there are others.

On which of these notions does relational grammar base itself? Apparently not on thematic relations; that much seems clear. What about the other two just mentioned? In *I promised John that I would leave,* does relational grammar consider *John* to be a direct object or an indirect object—or perhaps both at different levels? Suppose that we take *John* to be an indirect object. That would mean that at some abstract level of representation we have something analogous to *I promised to John that I would leave,* with a preposition between the verb and the noun.

At some other level *John* must be a direct object in the framework of relational grammar, because the passive can be applied: *John was promised that I would leave.* According to the principles of relational grammar, if I understand them, only a direct object can be "passivized," in other words, raised to subject. It is necessary to add a rule that turns an indirect object into a direct object. But such a rule seems completely ad hoc in this case.

M.R.:   Yes. After that, how can one prevent *Je parle à Jean* from becoming *Je parle Jean?*

N.C.:   I'm not sure. Suppose one takes *John* to be only a direct object in these sentences. In that case the relation is already expressed in terms of phrase markers, the syntactic structures. The direct object, in this sense, is the noun phrase in the configuration:

M.R.:   I heard Postal speak at the colloquium in Chicago in 1973; he sought to prove that the passive transformation is universal ... However, in general, it is not the grammatical rules which are universal, but the conditions imposed on the rules.

N.C.: I remain skeptical about the assumption that there is a rule of "passive," either in a single language or universally, across languages. In English it seems to me that there is good evidence for a transformational passive, a rule that moves a noun phrase to the subject position of the sentence or a noun phrase, giving such structures as *The city was destroyed* and *The city's destruction,* corresponding to *Destroy the city* and *Destruction of the city,* respectively. But this should not, I think, be regarded as a "rule of passive"; rather, it is a special case of a much more general rule of noun phrase (NP) movement that applies as well to derive such sentences as *John seems to be a nice fellow,* corresponding to *It seems that John is a nice fellow,* in which the NP-movement rule did not apply. To say that English has a "passive rule" seems to me insufficiently general. Rather, it has an NP-movement rule that happens to form passives, as a special case.

But "passive" does not seem to me a unitary phenomenon, either in a single language or across languages. Other languages use quite different means to achieve an effect similar to the English passive—which may be regarded, loosely, as a device to shift topic or to allow for subjectless sentences. In a language that uses, say, morphological devices in the construction roughly corresponding to English passive we would expect to find somewhat different properties for this construction.

In English, for example, the displaced noun phrase is not necessarily the direct object of the verb. To be sure, most frequently it is the direct object, as in *John saw Bill—Bill was seen by John.* But it can also be the notional indirect object: recall, *Bill was promised that I would leave.* Or again, this noun phrase may not have any relation to the main verb, as in *Believe (John to be a fool),* which can become *John was believed to be a fool.*

M.R.: In traditional terms, one says that the subject of the subordinate clause becomes the subject of the main clause.

N.C.:   In a language with a NP-movement rule we may also find that idiomatic expressions are subject to "passivization": corresponding to *Someone has taken advantage of Bill,* you have *Bill was taken advantage of* and *Advantage was taken of Bill.* Also, *Advantage seems to have been taken of Bill, Bill seems to have been taken advantage of,* and so on.

M.R.:   And one must not forget that the passive can be applied to what was formerly an indirect object: *Someone gave a book to John—Someone gave John a book—John was given a book.*

N.C.:   All these examples support the hypothesis that there is a rule displacing a noun phrase which follows the verb, independently of its function. One can go further. In his doctoral thesis, Joe Emonds argued plausibly that the rule forming passives is one of a general class of rules that are "structure-preserving" in the sense that the result of the transformation is a structure similar to those generated by the rewriting rules. Thus NP-movement places the displaced noun phrase in the subject position.

M.R.:   That is an important limitation. Otherwise it would seem a priori that transformations can generate structures of any kind.

N.C.:   Well, we see that the passive structure consists of the copula *be* followed by something like an adjective phrase. *John was seen* has a structure similar to *John was good. The door was closed* is ambiguous: either base-generated, like *The door was open,* or formed by NP-movement like *The door was opened.*

There are other properties of passivization that follow from quite general properties of movement rules. Fiengo has interesting things to say about this in his dissertation. There is a review of the matter in my book *Reflections on Language.*

In general, the passive construction in English exhibits a certain network of properties that follow from the assumption that a rule of NP-movement applies. In contrast, in many languages what corresponds roughly to English passive has different properties. There is a transitive verb construction with direct object, and a transitive verb may also appear with a different morphology with its direct object as subject. Contrary to the case in English, the subject of the passive form must be the direct object of the corresponding active form. It cannot be the subject of an embedded phrase, for example. Idiomatic expressions behave differently. There would be no reason to postulate a passive transformation for these languages: passive morphology is a lexical property of the verb.

In fact, it is not quite correct to say, as I just did, that there are two different types of language in this respect. It would be more accurate to say that there are two (and perhaps more) fundamental processes for forming what we informally call the "passive": one, transformational; the other, lexical. For example, English also has a lexical passive, as in one of the two senses of *The door was closed.* This lexical passive is perhaps clearer in negative structures like *untaught, unread,* etc. In *John was untaught,* or *The book was unread,* we must consider the passive as lexical, for quite general reasons, and not transformational—because in principle transformations may not generate lexical structures (this principle has been disputed, but I think it is correct). Note that in these cases the participles with the prefix *un-* behave exactly as predicted—like a lexical passive. We have *John was taught French* with the passive transformation, but not *John was untaught French,* because the lexical passive can only be formed with the direct object as the passive subject. Similarly we find lexical idiosyncrasies among the lexical passives, but not in the case of transformational passives, as the theory predicts. The meaning of *John was untaught, untutored,* is not predictable by means of a general rule from the meaning of *teach John, tutor John.* In the same way, the idiomatic expression *John was unread* certainly does not correspond to *read John.* But *John was taught French,* for example, has a meaning that is entirely predictable by a general rule as, in principle, in the case of true transformational rules: it has essentially the same meaning as *X taught John French.* These examples illustrate what seems to be a phenomenon of considerable generality. For reasons of principle rooted in the general theory of grammar, there are two quite different constructions called "passive," probably more.

I do not see any reason to suppose that there is a universal rule covering these distinct kinds of construction. To postulate a universal "rule of passive" would tend to obscure all these differences and also the general principles involved in their explication.

M.R.: French seems to be an intermediate case . . .

N.C.: French is an interesting case. I think the question requires more extensive study. For the moment it remains open.

CHAPTER 7

The Extended Standard Theory

M.R.: The theory which you propose at present is the Extended Standard Theory. A short time ago you mentioned that the contribution of Ray Jackendoff played a determining role in the elaboration of the new version of the model.

N.C.: By demonstrating the role of surface structure in semantic interpretation, yes. Contrary to what the Standard Theory of *Aspects* proposed, it seems highly probable that surface structure plays a primary role in semantic interpretation.

In fact, the sole—though essential—contribution of deep structure to determining the meaning of an expression seems to be the representation of so-called thematic relations, such as the relation of *key* to *open* as "instrument" in *John opened the door with a key, The key opened the door,* etc. The Extended Standard Theory assumes that the rewriting rules of the base generate deep structure in which lexical items are inserted. The thematic relations between the verb and the noun phrases which are grammatically related to it are defined at this level. Other semantic properties are determined by rules applying to surface structure. We have spoken of the co-reference of nouns and pronouns, where the relationships between positions in the surface structure appear to be decisive, and also of the interaction of negation and quantifiers. There too surface structure position is critical, a fact recognized in both the Extended

Standard Theory and generative semantics. There are other phenomena that relate to surface structure, for example, focus and presupposition.

M.R.:   Recently the Extended Standard Theory has incorporated a new concept, which seems most promising for syntax, semantics, and phonology: the concept of "trace." You define a trace *t* as a phonological zero element, which marks the position of an element that has been displaced by a transformation. For example:

> *Whom did you see?*—Whom did you see *t?* etc.

Lisa Selkirk, Thomas Wasow, and Robert Fiengo have shown the role of this in both phonology and semantics.

N.C.:   Within the framework of trace theory, one can even go further and say that *all* of semantic representation, including thematic relations, can in a sense be derived from surface structure: to be sure, with a considerably enriched notion of "surface structure," because the new surface structures contain traces, in terms of which thematic relations as specified by the base rules can be reconstructed.

M.R.:   In effect, the thematic relations say, for example, that the indirect object of the verb *teach* is a GOAL. That relation is preserved if the indirect object is displaced by a transformation. For example:

To whom   does Pierre   teach Latin
GOAL   AGENT   THEME

According to Jackendoff, the relation is displaced together with the noun. With trace theory (the trace being linked "as by an invisible thread" to the element which it replaced) one can attribute the thematic relation of the surface structure, because the order of the deep structure is still represented:

To whom   does   Pierre   teach   Latin   *t*
                 AGENT   THEME GOAL

N.C.:   *To whom* receives its thematic relation by the intervention of its trace.

M.R.:   The trace is a sort of memory of deep structure recorded in the surface structure.

N.C.:   From another point of view the trace in this case can be considered as indicating the position of a variable bound by a kind of quantifier which is introduced into the logical form by rules applying to the surface structure. In this latter version, the theory has roughly the following form: Deep structures are generated by the base component, with their specific properties. Transformations form surface structures enriched by traces. These surface structures are associated by further rules to representations of sound (phonetic representation) and meaning (logical form).

M.R.:   That gives the following schema:

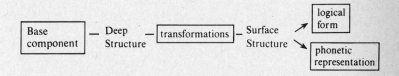

N.C.:   This is an alternative model of language as a cognitive system. Remember that by the phrase "logical form" I mean that partial representation of meaning that is determined by grammatical structure. Beyond that, we can study the interaction of this cognitive system with others, just as in physiology, once the heart has been identified, we can study its interaction with other organs.

M.R.:   It seems to me that you have chosen the expression "logical form" because all the semantic facts that depend on linguistic structure can be expressed in terms of traditional or modern logic.

N.C.:   I wouldn't want to imply that. Choice of the term *logical form* may or may not have been a wise terminological decision—the term is used in other ways. But terminology aside, there are interesting directions for research here. It has often been supposed (by me too) that the choice of logic used to express "logical form" is of no importance. For example, for thinking about quantifiers in natural language, any two logics having the same expressive power seemed to be equivalent. This seems reasonable if the relation between syntactic structure and logical form is taken to be expressed by a principle that applies in "one step," as it were. But in the model we are sketching out now, the derivation of logical form proceeds step by step. Logical form is determined by a derivational process analogous to those of syntax and phonology. Then the choice of logical notation becomes crucial. It is possible that certain rules will be stated properly at an intermediate level in terms of one logic and not in terms of another; and this appears to be the case. For example, a logic with variables and a logic without variables have the same expressive power. But if the logical form is derived step by step, it turns out that a logic with variables is required to express certain general principles which explain facts of language. Consequently, it becomes possible to obtain empirical evidence to answer the question: Which is the correct system of logic, the notation actually used in mental representation?

There is interesting evidence suggesting that the right logic is a classical logic with variables. Perhaps we can explain in these terms why classical logic with variables is so intuitive. We can consider it to be, in effect, a simplified version, somewhat schematized, of the logical form determined by surface structure. It can virtually be "read off the mind." In contrast, logical systems without variables, even though they often have the same expressive power, are more counterintuitive, and are generally understood more readily through the mediation of classical logic. It can also be shown, I believe, that they simply do not furnish the types of representation appropriate for formulating rules that relate the surface structure to the logical form in the most general way.

Montague's theory of quantification is one such case. The situation with respect to the choice of a logic is in a certain way comparable to familiar problems in phonology. Thus, two systems of distinctive features can have the same "expressive power" in principle, but one might be preferred to the other—and we can conclude that it is correct for language, and the other false—because one permits the formulation of certain generalizations and explanatory principles while the other doesn't. The situation seems to me to be the same with regard to the relation of surface structure to logical form. As far as I can see, certain significant generalizations require a classical logic containing variables, where at times the variables reflect the presence of a trace in surface structure.

M.R.: That is what you talked about in your lecture at Vincennes. It seems to me that these recent discoveries also explain the history of the relations between logic and language theory. Before generative grammar, all those who wanted to account for the languages in a somewhat systematic manner turned to logic to furnish them a "generative base." That was true of certain structuralists—here I'm thinking of Šaumjan—and it was true of the grammatical tradition.

The first act of generative grammar was to separate itself from that tradition. You said: Though logic is necessary for the construction of scientific theory, the syntax of natural languages is not reducible to logic. No, deep structure is not the logical structure of propositions; and so on. The theory of syntax elaborates its own concepts.

However, one question remained: If the structure of language does not depend on logical structure, *how is it possible that generations of philosophers could speak of these questions and work on them to such an extent,* and understand each other? How does one explain this "intuition" of which you speak? The hypothesis of a "logical form" as a component interpreting surface structure could answer that question; philosophers and grammarians have never studied the properties of surface structure, even though they thought they saw deep structures there. The Port-Royal *Grammaire Générale* analyzed the sentence, *Dieu invisible a créé le monde visible* into the propositions *Dieu est invisible,* etc. It was thought that the complex of these propositions constituted the deep structure of the sentence. Now it is the opposite that is true: deep structure is a part of syntactic structure, and the complex of propositions is deduced from *interpretive rules* belonging to the semantic component, which give a "content" to the surface structure. It is therefore hardly astonishing that logical form is related to surface structure. But the point of view is altogether different.

N.C.: Completely. Not long ago I thought that there was no sense to the question whether, say, traditional logic with variables or Montague's theory of quantifiers, for example, is the *right* logic, the logic that is in fact employed in logical form and plays a part in explaining semantic properties of language. But that was incorrect. The fact that it is possible to find empirical arguments bearing on this question in itself constitutes an interesting result.

CHAPTER 8

Deep Structure

M.R.:   Perhaps by retracing the history of deep structure we can take up that of generative grammar again, this time from another viewpoint?

N.C.:   If you like. Let us begin with that phrase: the term *deep structure* itself was proposed in the context of the Standard Theory. Recall that this theory proposed the existence of a class of structures:

—which were generated by the rules of the base component;

—which received semantic interpretation;

—which were converted by transformations into well-formed surface structures.

M.R.:   And which contained the lexical items.

N.C.:   Yes. This was the point at which lexical items were inserted. It was thus simply a technical term.

However, the expression had been used in other ways. For example, Wittengenstein had used the distinction *deep grammar-surface grammar.* Hockett adopted similar terminology in his *Course of Modern Linguistics.* What they had in mind was the distinction between things which are not presented directly and those which are.

Whorf made use of the notion "covert categories," that is, categories which have a functional role with no morphological reflection.

The point is that similar expressions had already appeared in the literature. Speaking of generative grammar, however, one must use the term in its technical sense, putting aside loose associations of ideas or more or less vague similarities.

In the earlier version of the theory, say, in *LSLT,* there was no concept of "deep structure." The concept closest to it was the technical notion *T-marker.* This determined the semantic representation. This T-marker represented the transformational history of sentences, just as the P-marker (phrase marker) represented a derivational history of rewriting rules. Remember that first model. It was supposed that rewriting rules generate a finite number of abstract objects, which could be transformed into surface structures by "singulary" transformations operating to form a simple sentence; thus one obtained a finite class of "kernel sentences" such as *John said that, Bill has just come in;* and also simple derived sentences such as *This book has been read by everyone in England,* etc.

"Generalized" transformations embedded certain structures within others: *John said that Bill has just come in,* etc.

The arrangement of these singulary and generalized transformations formed the transformational history represented by the T-marker. This marker consequently showed how sentences are associated with one another, what are the relations among their parts, and so on. It is in this respect that it can be compared to deep structure.

In the version that followed next, the term *deep structure* was in some ways "overdetermined": we have seen that in the Standard Theory it is generated by the base, receives the lexical items and undergoes semantic interpretation, and, finally, is converted to well-formed surface structure. It is important to note that these properties are independent. The structure which undergoes semantic interpretation is not necessarily the one which is the locus of lexical insertion, or which is transformed into surface structure.

In fact, the work which followed *Aspects* distinguished these different properties and showed that they had to be dissociated.

The Extended Standard Theory maintains that it is not the deep structure which undergoes semantic interpretation. We have seen that under trace theory one can say that surface structure is associated directly with semantic representation.

What happened to the concept of "deep structure" is what happens in the development of any theory. Terms are defined within a particular context, and this context changes as people construct different empirical hypotheses. The terms then take on a different meaning.

Take the term *atom:* that term does not signify today what it meant for the Greeks. Concepts change constantly as the theoretical matrix changes. In the natural sciences no one fails to understand that—at least not to too great a degree. But in a field like linguistics it bothers people enormously. The only thing we can do is try to preserve the clarity of ideas.

For some, "deep structure" continues to mean that structure which bears semantic representation.

M.R.:   Following generative semantics . . .

N.C.:   More or less. I have continued to use the term for the structure generated by the base, which is transformed into well-formed surface structure. The source of confusion lies in the fact that we employ the same term in two different senses.

However, the greatest confusion comes from people working at the periphery of the field, for example, some literary critics who use the term in a vaguely Wittgensteinian sense. Many people have attributed the word *deep* to grammar itself, perhaps identifying "deep structure" and "universal grammar."

I have read many criticisms saying how ill-conceived it is to postulate innate deep structures. I never said that, and nothing I have written suggests anything of the sort, though such a view has been maintained by others.

Similarly, I have often read that what I am proposing is that deep structures do not vary from one language to another, that all languages have the same deep structure: people have apparently been misled by the word *deep* and confuse it with *invari-*

ant. Once again, the only thing I claim to be "invariant" is universal grammar.

M.R.:   In *Reflections on Language* you replace the term *deep structure* with *initial phrase marker.*

N.C.:   To try to avoid precisely those confusions we've just mentioned. But if people want to be confused, they will always succeed, no matter what term you use. The expression "initial phrase marker" has the advantage of sounding like a technical term. Yet it can still be misleading: how is one going to interpret "initial"? As earliest in time? That would be senseless.

M.R.:   Furthermore, the fact that semantics has been linked to deep structure . . .

N.C.:   . . . has made people think that everything "deep" must relate to semantics. People think that semantics must be something "deep." Again an association that provokes misunderstandings. We come back to the question of the different ways in which things can be interesting or intellectually "deep."

Semantics seems deep in part because it remains obscure. That does not necessarily mean that it really is a deep subject. Perhaps it is trivial and we don't yet recognize that. Perhaps there is nothing very interesting to understand. To be sure, semantics is interesting in itself. But on the intellectual level it may turn out that phonology requires extremely abstract rules that enter into complex deductions and explain a large number of phenomena. In that sense phonology is deep—as physics is deep. Is semantics "deep" in that sense? For the moment the answer is no. To merit the term *deep,* a subject must provide answers to certain questions that attain a certain level of intellectual depth. But all this has nothing to do with the technical notion "deep structure."

M.R.:   And then too, the work of Joan Bresnan (which shows that the accentuation of English sentences must take into consideration not only surface structure, but also deep and intermediary structures) destroys the idea that the phonological aspect of language only involves the surface . . .

N.C.:   That's true, and that is another aspect of the Standard Theory that has been properly criticized.

M.R.:   In the Standard Theory we have a symmetry of relations: deep structure–semantic interpretation, and surface structure–phonological interpretation.

N.C.:   Today it seems that a different schema may be necessary: surface structure determines semantic representation—that is, in the enriched sense of surface structure in which certain properties of underlying deep structure are captured by means of trace theory.

M.R.:   And deep structure may determine the phonology. That would give:

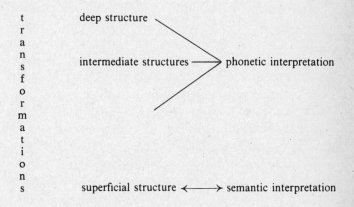

N.C.:   But that's not all. Another property attributed to the deep structure in the Standard Theory has been questioned. That is the idea that it expresses *all* the grammatical relations among lexical items. Take the thesis of Jean-Roger Vergnaud on relative clauses.[1] He puts forward the hypothesis that in a sentence containing a relative clause, the noun phrase which appears in the main clause is in fact "raised" from the relative clause. For example, the sentence *I saw the man who was there* is derived from a deep structure like

$$I \; saw \; (\!- \; (the \; man \; was \; there)).$$
$$NP \qquad\quad S$$

The noun phrase *the man* is taken from the embedded clause and placed in the NP position left empty to the right of the verb in the main clause. Under this hypothesis a noun phrase is left empty in the deep structure and a noun is inserted in this structure by a transformational rule. That would imply that the grammatical relation (hence the thematic relation) between *see* and *man* is not determined in the deep structure. The grammatical relation between the structural positions is determined by the deep structure, but not the relation between the lexical elements. So here we have again an interesting idea modifying the definition of deep structure.

Carlos Otero has advanced an interesting idea that is more radical. He suggests that lexical insertion takes place altogether in surface structure. Why? For one thing, because transformations never refer to the phonetic properties of words. If words enter into the structure at the level of surface structure, this fact would be explained. This theory predicts that the idiosyncratic* properties of words do not have any effect on transformations, which seems to be true.

This hypothesis is particularly interesting for those languages where inflectional morphology has considerable effect on the internal structure of words. In English that only happens in the case of irregular words. But when the regular morphological forms vary greatly, one might want to say that the word is generated in the form in which it appears in the surface structure. Other considerations are also relevant. The question remains open, but if the answer is positive, then surface structure is the locus of lexical insertion.

M.R.:   Sometimes the word *deep* is accorded value for reasons just as bad as those for which it has been criticized. People

---

*A particular property of each word which distinguishes it from other words. See also p.136.

see the possibility of a new hermeneutics here. This is actually the same mistake . . .

N.C.:   Yes, in terms of things that are "hidden," that are to be discovered; but there are many aspects of phonology that are "deep" in this sense of the word.

M.R.:   The word *surface** is equally misleading . . .

N.C.:   Surface structure is something quite abstract, involving properties that do not appear in the physical form . . . It is by virtue of such properties that language is worth studying.

M.R.:   Personally I find quite fascinating an abstraction or depth that is linked to trace theory—that is, *the astonishing study of the structuring effect of silence:* in phonology, the trace changes the intonation; in semantics, it blocks co-reference . . .

N.C.:   That is a really interesting property of surface structures.

M.R.:   In poetry too, in metrics, these structuring silences are essential . . . But don't you think that by placing so much stress on surface structure, you invite being accused of returning to structuralism? In general, whenever you have refined a concept, you have been accused of abandoning your fundamental hypotheses. I remember reading that your definition of degrees of grammaticalness signifies that you have abandoned the concept of grammaticalness!

N.C.:   Well, in fact, the notion of "degree of grammaticalness" was developed at the same time as the notion of "grammaticalness," within the theory of generative grammar, that is, in the early 1950s. A chapter of *LSLT* is devoted to this question, and I also refer to it in *Syntactic Structures.* But what is more important is that the kind of criticism you're referring to reveals once again the difference between the attitude of the natural sciences on the one hand, and one often found in the social sciences and "humanities" on the other. The latter, which lack the intellectual content of the natural sciences, are to a great degree involved with personalities rather than ideas. In science it is self-evident that concepts are going to change; that

---

*"Superficiel" in French, thus even more so—Translator.

is just to say that you hope to learn something. This is not theology, after all. You do not make declarations which you must preserve unchanged for the rest of your life. By contrast, in the social sciences or in humanistic studies, positions are often personalized. Once you have taken a position, you are supposed to defend it no matter what happens. The positions of one or another school are identified with individuals. It becomes a question of honor not to change, that is, to learn nothing. In linguistics that is very striking: you are accused of refuting yourself if you modify your position. I have often read such criticism, and I find it difficult to comprehend.

If you are concerned to discover the truth, whether you work alone or in a group, it is evident that you are going to change your mind often—each time an issue of a serious journal appears. When there is real progress, these changes will be significant. You come to think in a different way. The first approximations have to be changed to other approximations, better ones.

As far as the alleged "return to structuralism" is concerned: first of all, suppose that were true—fine! It often happens that hypotheses in the natural sciences are abandoned at a certain period because they are inadequate, but are then reconstructed later when a higher level of comprehension has been attained. Take the theory of the atom: abandoned, then resurrected in a different form. That does not mean that we have returned to Democritus! Not at all. Things progress, new perspectives open up, reinterpreting what was previously rejected. There is no "personal defeat" in that.

Take the question of Cartesianism. It was entirely correct to abandon the Cartesian doctrine for a long time. I think it is correct to return to something like it today, but in a substantially different form.

M.R.:   It does not seem to me that in the case of surface structure we have a return to whatever it may have been.

N.C.:   The work of the last ten years has shown that surface structure plays a role which was not suspected previously. Can one therefore speak of a return to structuralism? In my opinion, that does not make any sense in this case. The technical concept of surface structure did not really exist in structuralist theories, and recent theories raise a large number of questions concerning surface structure that could not have been posed within the structuralist framework. That concept, in the current sense, appeared only with generative grammar, as an infinite class of structures . . .

M.R.: It is defined by its opposition to *deep structure,* etc.

N.C.: And as I've said, a surface structure which incorporates traces is much more abstract than the earlier notion. Thus we have a concept of surface structure defined in terms of rules that generate an infinite set of objects, standing in opposition to deep structure, and considerably more abstract than before, in that properties of deep structure are captured through trace theory.

On the other hand, suppose one were to discover that the structuralist concept of phoneme plays a very important role, previously unsuspected. Suppose that the arguments that have been advanced against the existence of a phonemic level could be surmounted within another conceptual framework. That would not be a return to an old idea, but an advance to a new idea, giving a new significance to an old concept. That would be progress.

When theories and the concepts that appear in them are personalized, one looks to see "who" is wrong; but that is not the correct way of thinking. That "who" may have been right in the context of his or her own time, wrong in the context of a richer theory, and will perhaps prove right once again. That's fine. Furthermore, there is nothing wrong with being wrong. Progress is based on interesting ideas which generally prove wrong—either incomplete, misconstrued, or completely wrong.

M.R.: In the humanities certain professors spend their time in effect teaching their Ph.D. thesis.

N.C.: Anybody who teaches at age fifty what he was teaching at age twenty-five had better find another profession. If in twenty-five years nothing has happened which proves to you that your ideas were wrong, it means that you are not in a living field, or perhaps are part of a religious sect.

M.R.: In a field where you are only asked to *apply* a theory to a new object, this kind of sclerosis can also appear. Within the framework of structuralist phonology, for example, you are offered a method for finding the phonological system of a language, and when you have found it, the work is completed. In generative phonology, that is where the work begins . . .

N.C.: Structuralist phonology—quite apart from the question of its validity—posed rather limited questions. And as you say, once you have answered these questions, the interesting work can begin.

That aspect of structuralism troubled me when I was a student. I liked linguistics very much, it was intriguing. But it was not too clear what the point was; in a sense the discipline was closed. Suppose one had completed the phonemic analysis of all the languages in the world, as well as the morphological analysis and analysis of constituents, in the sense of structuralist methodology. These are finite systems (with some ambiguity in the latter case), analyzable according to procedures that were taken to be essentially perfected, except for some details, and which were applicable to any language. Such a field is hardly worth the trouble of exploring. Rather like in natural history: imagine that you have described all the butterflies . . .

M.R.: On this point structuralist linguistics is deceptive, just as is the way it is taught. What do the professors ask of students? To apply a ready-made method. One is condemned to repeat what has already been established. Personally, my enthusiasm for linguistics was born largely at the moment when I understood that it offered a means to do intellectual *and* creative work within the "humanities." Instead, in literary studies and in the human and social sciences students were asked to apply methods without any reflection . . .

Certainly, the intellectual creativity inherent in generative grammar is also based on rules, but those are explicit rules which one can challenge or change.

N.C.: Furthermore, if some field is still at the level where procedural methods can be applied, then it is at a very primitive level indeed. A purely descriptive level, say, like Babylonian astronomy, or not even that. There are no "methods" in this sense in a field having real intellectual content. The goal is to find the truth. How to do that, nobody knows. There are no procedures that can be outlined in advance for discovering scientific truth. You cannot train a creative physicist or biologist by telling him: "Here are the methods, apply them to a new organism." That may be the way to train a lab technician, but not a scientist. You do that when you don't know how to find meaningful work for students. It is an admission of failure.

What you expect of a scientist is to discover new principles, new theories, even new modes of verification ... That won't happen by learning a fixed procedure. The same is true of linguistics today. It is impossible to explain to someone the procedure he must apply in order to find the generative grammar of some language. What one looks forward to is the discovery of new phenomena that will show that the theories which have been proposed are false, that they must be changed—new questions that no one has thought of posing before, at least in a clear manner, new contributions to understanding, achieved perhaps with new "methods." And finally, new ideas and new principles, which will reveal how limited, false, and superficial are the assumptions that we hold to be valid today.

M.R.: At times that may disturb students accustomed to traditional instruction, where it is sufficient to learn passively what you are taught. In generative grammar, in effect, instruction consists in the explication of fundamental concepts, and in the presentation of the history of the discipline in terms of a detailed account of different hypotheses. One can explain the manner in which something is demonstrated, how such a demonstration is constructed. But one cannot tell anyone how to find a new idea, how to invent. Invention is linked to the *desire* to understand one's chosen field better.

CHAPTER 9

Universal Grammar and Unresolved Questions

M.R.: These last years you have concentrated your linguistic work on the discovery of the *conditions imposed on rules,* that is, hypotheses concerning universal grammar. This is the third epoch of generative grammar which I defined at the beginning.

N.C.: We may think of universal grammar as the system of principles which characterizes the class of possible grammars by specifying how particular grammars are organized (what are the components and their relations), how the different rules of these components are constructed, how they interact, and so on.

M.R.: It is a sort of metatheory.

N.C.: And a set of empirical hypotheses bearing on the biologically determined language faculty. The task of the child learning a language is to choose from among the grammars provided by the principles of universal grammar that grammar which is compatible with the limited and imperfect data presented to him. That is to say, once again, that language acquisition is not a step-by-step process of generalization, association, and abstraction, going from linguistic data to the grammar, and that the subtlety of our understanding transcends by far what is presented in experience.

M.R.: The expression "mental organ" has appeared on occasion in these hypotheses . . .

N.C.: I think that is a correct and useful analogy, for reasons we have already discussed. The problems concerning this "mental organ" are very technical, perhaps too much so to enter into detail here. A particular grammar includes rewriting rules, transformational rules, lexical rules, rules of semantic and phonological interpretation. It seems that there are several components in a grammar, several classes of rules, each having specific properties, linked in a manner determined by the principles of universal grammar. The theory of universal grammar has as its goal to determine precisely the nature of each of these components of the grammar and their interaction. For reasons we have already discussed—having to do with the uniformity of acquisition of a highly complex and articulated structure on the basis of limited data—we can be sure that universal grammar, once we have understood it correctly, imposes severe restrictions on the variety of possible rule systems. But this means that the permissible rules cannot express in detail how they function, and it also means that the rules tend to overgenerate —one cannot include *within the rules themselves* the restrictions placed on their application. What many linguists have tried to do is to abstract from the rules some quite general principles that govern their application. The study of these abstract conditions is a particularly interesting part of universal grammar. I have been working on this topic since the beginning of the 1960s, and more specifically in the past few years. From about 1970, I have been working on and writing about some fairly radical hypotheses on this subject.

These hypotheses restrict very severely the expressive power of transformational rules, thereby limiting the class of possible transformational grammars. To compensate for the fact that the rules, thus restricted, tend to generate far too many structures, several quite general principles have been proposed concerning the manner in which transformational rules must be applied to given structures. These general principles are of a very natural type, in my opinion, associated with quite reasonable constraints on information processing, in ways that are probably related quite closely to the language faculty. What I hope to be able to show is that these principles provide the basic framework for "mental computation," and that in interaction with rules of limited variety and expressive power, they suffice to explain the curious arrangement of phenomena that we discover when we study in detail how sentences are formed, used, and understood. I doubt that they will work entirely, but I believe that they are on the right track. This type of approach has proven very productive, much more so than I expected. In my opinion this is a reasonable way to develop the Extended Standard Theory. Some work has been published, and more is on the way. I feel that the work of the past few years is much more encouraging than has been the case for quite some time. I'm very happy about it . . .

M.R.:   That is obvious, in any case . . .

N.C.:   Yes, I feel that we are getting somewhere. I hope that I'll be able to find the time . . .

M.R.:   However, these recent results, unlike what was done previously in semantics, for example, were not foreseen in the initial program of *LSLT*. These are new kinds of problems.

N.C.:   Considerably different. The theory presented in *LSLT* permitted a great number of rules. I tried at first to provide a system rich enough to express as much as I could imagine. Now, in a sense, I'm trying to do the opposite, to limit the expressive power of the rules. In *LSLT* there is no distinction between rules and conditions on rules. That distinction appeared first in *Current Issues in Linguistic Theory,* with the A/A condition,* the principle of recoverability of deletion, and a certain number of others, proposed as conditions belonging

---

*This condition hypothesizes that a constituent of the category A cannot be extracted from within another constituent of the same category A. This prevented, for example, the complement of a noun contained within a direct object from being chosen as the NP displaced by the passive transformation:

(a) *John saw ((Mary)'s brother)*
       NP   NP
(b) *Mary was seen brother by John*

to universal grammar. Ross developed this approach in an original and very important way in his thesis, as did others. A recent book by Richard Kayne on French syntax is a particularly important contribution in this direction. This line of research has proven very productive.

M.R.: Many misunderstandings have surrounded your reference to universal grammar. Some have even taken it to be a universal language. In my opinion this is due to the fact that it is very difficult to imagine what a condition imposed on a rule is, without knowing what linguistic structure is . . .

N.C.: . . . And without knowing what a rule is, yes.

M.R.: For that a minimum knowledge of linguistics is required. Otherwise one imagines "spontaneously"—that is to say, due to the philosophic tradition internalized through the mediation of the contemporary vocabulary—that universal grammar is like logic. That is why so often one has seen very different kinds of people confuse "universal grammar" with "deep structure," because by "deep structure" they understand the logical subject-predicate proposition, supposed by philosophers as underlying all language. This confusion is impossible in generative grammar. Universal grammar is a sort of metatheory; deep structure, as we have seen, is a technical term pertaining to the particular grammar, and designating a precise stage in the derivation of a sentence.

N.C.: In the same fashion, some philosophers have objected that human beings do not have "innate grammars"—as they think I have proposed. This is simply to confuse universal grammar with grammar. It is important to keep in mind that universal grammar is not a grammar, but rather a theory of grammars, a kind of metatheory or schematism for grammar. In that sense, the theory presented in *LSLT* or in any general book on linguistic theory is an attempt to formulate the principles of universal grammar, at least in the sense in which I am using the expression "universal grammar." As linguistic work progresses, we can hope that it will lead to a deeper understanding of "universal grammar," that is, linguistic theory, with the constraints this theory imposes on what counts as a possible human language.

As you have remarked, much of the work of the past few years has been concentrated on universal grammar in a more clear-cut and sharper fashion than before. The difference, of course, is "quantitative," insofar as every formulation of linguistic theory is intended as a contribution to universal grammar. But the remark is correct in that there has been, I believe, some real progress toward formulating the principles of universal grammar, at least in the domain of syntax and phonology (much less in semantics, where research has not yet produced principles of any substantial scope or explanatory power). But as you emphasize correctly, universal grammar in the sense in which the term is used in the work on generative grammar must not be confused with deep structure.

Unresolved Questions

M.R.:   Today many linguists are working within the framework of generative grammar, and on all kinds of languages. This theory has already permitted the discovery and explanation of a large number of facts; in general, the results of this work are accessible to anyone who wishes to take the trouble to read them. However, in spite of the number of positive results, I imagine that many questions are still without an answer.

N.C.:   Certainly! But it is useful to distinguish two types of questions: internal questions and external questions. By internal questions I mean those that arise from the moment when you begin to work within a particular version of linguistic theory, for example, the Extended Standard Theory. By external questions I mean those concerning the choice of this general type of theory instead of others based on quite different assumptions, the epistemological status of the theory, the problem of the legitimacy of its idealizations, the interactions with other systems, and so on.

As far as internal questions are concerned, they are innumerable. They arise whenever you attempt to test the theory you have formulated and try to improve it; there is no interesting hypothesis, to my knowledge, which is not confronted by counterexamples that are very serious—for example, the conditions on rules, such as the specified subject condition.* In my opinion, some of these hypotheses are reasonably well substantiated. Nevertheless, when you study complex linguistic material, a large number of phenomena do not seem to obey these conditions, others seem to obey different conditions, and still others do not follow any conditions that have been proposed.

To be concrete, take "reflexivation." That is a process which varies from one language to another. In English reflexivation works rather like bound anaphora, that is, the kind of anaphora that one finds in sentences like *John lost his way,* where *his* must obligatorily refer back to *John.* (By contrast, in *John lost his book* there is no bound anaphora, because here *his* can refer to anyone, including *John.*)

The idea of treating reflexivation as a case of bound anaphora is due to Michael Helke, who developed it in his Ph.D. thesis at MIT several years ago. It seems to me quite correct, for English and for a number of other languages. According to this view, reflexives are a special case of bound anaphora. Therefore, *John hurts himself* is analogous to *John lost his way.* And more generally, the conditions which hold for bound anaphora apply also to reflexivation.

However, even in English, this matter is not at all clear. Thus, many speakers accept such sentences as *The pictures of themselves that I gave them are hanging in the library, They thought that some pictures of themselves would be on exhibit,* and so on. In his book Jackendoff gives many complicated examples of varying degrees of acceptability; a number have been suggested by others too. These facts raise many problems.

*See above, p. 61.

Furthermore, in other languages reflexivation has very different properties; this is true in Korean, for example. While in English the antecedent of the reflexive must be found in the same sentence, in Korean the form that seems to correspond most closely to the English reflexive can refer to something not mentioned in the sentence at all. This has been studied by Wha-Chun Kim in a recent MIT dissertation. The phenomenon is obscured by certain rules which tend to choose an antecedent nearer to the reflexive pronoun, but it seems that these are rules of preference, and in fact reflexives can refer back to something given in common knowledge or previous discourse. In such a language the rules of reflexivation do not seem to belong to the sentence grammar in the strict sense: the rule which governs the form that is comparable to the English reflexive seems rather to be a rule of "discourse," or to be more exact, a rule which relates linguistic competence to the other cognitive systems that play a role in performance.

There are also languages where the behavior of what is considered to be the reflexive is different from the case of either English or Korean. For example, Polish, Japanese, perhaps Classical Greek. In these languages the reflexive must be bound to something in the same sentence, it appears, but not under the restrictive conditions governing English reflexive—rather, some very general conditions on anaphora, involving domination, grammatical relation, and perhaps linear precedence apply.*

If you want to ask embarrassing questions, you can ask me what all this means. Does it mean that reflexivation can be simply anything? Certainly not. Do these different classes of reflexives have common properties? Are they governed by other principles of anaphora? Are they similar to reciprocal pronouns? How do they behave with respect to the conditions on rules? In many cases they violate conditions on rules which seem valid otherwise. Is it that we do not know how to formu-

---

*See pp. 181–82.

late the rules governing the reflexive, or is it that the conditions on rules are wrong, or is there some other reason? All these remain open questions.

For virtually everything that has been studied seriously, questions of this nature arise. To answer them, one might undertake investigations of a wide range of languages. I'm not sure that that is likely to be the most productive approach. If the conditions in question are at a certain level of abstraction, then no "phenomenon" will confirm or refute them; only rules can do so. Therefore one must begin by establishing a system of rules to see if they are compatible with the conditions. The phenomena in themselves tell us nothing about the validity of a condition on rules. They bear on the condition only indirectly, to the extent to which the phenomena corroborate a system of rules that can be evaluated with respect to its conformity to the postulated conditions. One cannot verify a condition by referring to a traditional grammar, or by asking an informant. Serious work on particular languages shows how difficult it is to establish a correct rule. Only too often one's early assumptions prove wrong. This does not mean that these abstract conditions on rules cannot be falsified; it means that one must work quite seriously on a language before it is possible to argue that a condition is falsified or verified.

The problem is quite general. A particular language must be studied in depth before facts and arguments emerge which have real theoretical significance. You can always look at a language and make some observations: "Here are the cases, the relations, etc." That does not mean much. Because when we study the problem closely, what seems true on the surface may be quite misleading. These internal questions may not be easy to resolve; they require hard work. One must study a language in considerable depth to find the facts that bear on principles of any significance.

Serious questions arise concerning the attitude one should take toward apparent counterexamples. At what point must they be taken seriously? In the natural sciences apparent counterevidence is often ignored, on the assumption that it will somehow be taken care of later. That is quite a sane attitude. Within reasonable limits, of course, not to excess. Because we must recognize that our comprehension of nontrivial phenomena is always extremely limited. That is true in physics and far more true in linguistics. We understand only fragments of reality, and we can be sure that every interesting and significant theory is at best only partially true. That is not a reason for abandoning theories or abandoning rational research.

At a given moment one has to cut short the questions that arise. One must try to assess the relative importance of the phenomena or rules that contradict one's hypotheses, as compared with the evidence supporting them. Then, one will either put aside counterevidence to be dealt with later, or else decide that the theory is inadequate and must be reconstructed. The choice isn't easy. There is no algorithm. And as this kind of problem arises constantly in the course of research, it is an intuitive judgment whether or not one should persevere within a given framework—because of the positive results and in spite of the apparent counterexamples. In general, there has been considerable progress in linguistics, if one considers the positive results—even if innumerable problems remain at each stage. "Methodologists" sometimes assert that a counterexample serves to refute a theory and shows that it must be abandoned. Such an injunction finds little support in the practice of the advanced sciences, as is well known, virtually a truism, in the history of science. The willingness to put aside the counterexamples to a theory with some degree of explanatory force, a theory that provides a degree of insight, and to take them up again at a higher level of understanding, is quite simply the path of rationality. In fact, it constitutes the precondition for significant progress in any nontrivial field of research.

M.R.:   And the external questions?

N.C.:   With respect to those, there are quite a few that one must keep in mind. For example, there is the question of the autonomy of syntax, which opposes formal grammar to "full" grammar. Is this an appropriate abstraction? Is it correct to say that the concepts of phonology and syntax are defined on the basis of formal primitive notions and not semantic primitives? Or is the distinction a proper one in the first place?

M.R.: We have seen that generative grammar replies "yes" to this question.

N.C.: At least certain tendencies within generative grammar. This answer seems to me to be the correct one, with certain qualifications. But one must not forget that these are important questions. In the same way, one may question the legitimacy of the idealization to language in the first place. Is it legitimate to say that grammar is a mechanism which associates phonetic representation and logical form? Does such a system really exist? Is one saying something correct about the human mind when one postulates that there is a mental organ consisting of a system of rules relating phonetic representation to logical form through the mechanism of syntax? That assumption involves a commitment to the legitimacy of a certain idealization. But of course we don't suppose that there is a box inside the brain. What this idealization means has often been misunderstood.

One can maintain with Ross and Lakoff, for example, that such a system does not exist, that grammatical rules must take into account personal beliefs and attitudes. If they are right, grammar constitutes an illegitimate idealization. I don't feel that there is justification for this position, but the question cannot be brushed aside a priori.

To demonstrate the legitimacy of an abstraction, it must be shown in the first place that it leads to interesting results. Then one must indicate how it is integrated within a more general schema. On this subject, just about everything remains to be done. How can a model of competence be integrated within performance models, models of speaking, and perception? To develop a model of performance, a model of competence must be presupposed; it is difficult to imagine a coherent alternative. It remains to be shown how knowledge of language is put to use. However, if for the moment there are no other plausible approaches, that does not mean they will never exist.

Finally, the physical realization of all these systems, of competence and of performance, remains quite unknown. We can only speak in a very abstract manner about properties of the mind. What are the physical mechanisms that satisfy the abstract conditions that we are now able to study? What corresponds physically to these systems and properties about which we make hypotheses? These are fundamental questions. Very little is known about the physical bases of these systems.

M.R.:   Can one consider as "external" the questions posed by sociolinguistics?

N.C.:   It is conceivable. I'm not sure what these questions are. One can imagine that the definition of a language or a dialect could be one such question. It seems doubtful that these are really linguistic notions.

What is the "Chinese language"? Why is "Chinese" called a language and the Romance languages, different languages? The reasons are political, not linguistic. On purely linguistic grounds, there would be no reason to say that Cantonese and Mandarin are dialects of one language while Italian and French are different languages. Furthermore, what makes French a single language? I suppose fifty years ago neighboring villages could be found which spoke dialects of French sufficiently different so that mutual intelligibility was limited.

So what is a language? There is a standard joke that a language is a dialect with an army and a navy. These are not linguistic concepts. As for other questions of sociolinguistics, it does not seem clear to me that they have been posed in a way that permits serious answers, for reasons that we have already discussed.

M.R.:   The linguistic concept is *grammar*.

N.C.:   Sociolinguistics is presumably concerned not with grammars in the sense of our discussion, but rather with concepts of a different sort, among them, perhaps, "language," if such a notion can become an object of serious study. As I've already said, it seems to me that any such study should be based on the idealization to systems in idealized homogeneous communities. Beyond that, it is not very clear that there are significant principles governing the extent and character of the variability of the system or systems in the heads of speakers or members of a language community.

Questions of language are basically questions of *power,* the kind of exercise of power that created the system of nation-states as in Europe. Plainly, this is not the only system of political organization. For example, in the old Ottoman Empire, regions such as the Levant incorporated numerous local communities, related to each other in various ways, and with a good deal of linguistic variation as well. Nobody spoke the Classical Arabic taught in the schools, but the so-called dialects were considered inferior. The intervention of the Western imperial powers led to a system of states, leaving bitter and unresolved conflicts and antagonisms, a system in which each individual must define himself as belonging to a nation or a *nation-state.* It is a system imposed from the outside on a region ill-adapted to it. Much the same is true in Africa, where the intrusion of the imperial powers has imposed a framework of *national* organization that does not correspond to the earlier nature of these societies. Consolidation of nation-states, as earlier in Europe, interacts in complex ways with the spread of national languages. There are no doubt important questions here, but it doesn't seem obvious that linguistics has much to contribute to the investigation of them.

M.R.:   What you have just said allows me to turn the accusation certain sociolinguists have made against generative grammar back against them. They called linguistics "imperialistic" because it was preoccupied with idealized systems, and in particular with standard systems, the study of which has been facilitated by prior researches. In short, what these critics want is that one studies the *language* of the people. You have just indicated to what extent that notion originated with bourgeois power, and in particular, with imperialism!

N.C.:   I can't see that the charge makes any sense, for reasons we've already discussed—that the perfect speaker of an idealized system does not exist in the real world. In the speech of real speakers idealized systems interact; each of us speaks a variety of these systems, intermingling them in a complex fashion. Because the experience of individuals is different, the mixture of systems is different. But I do not believe that outside these systems there exists a reality of *dialect* or *language.*

Perhaps I am wrong. Perhaps there are constraints on the ways in which linguistic systems can or cannot enter into interaction in a single community, or a wider group, or the mind of a single person. Perhaps we shall find that certain combinations are possible and others impossible. If principles emerge which govern the interaction of these systems, then these will belong to a field called sociolinguistics. Perhaps one may also find a way to relate these principles to principles of sociology . . . No doubt, in social interaction all sorts of questions involve language. Perhaps the study of these questions will draw upon and in turn influence linguistic studies in some significant way. It is conceivable. I'm personally skeptical.

The situation is very different as far as the connection between language and cognitive psychology is concerned. Here there are questions with a fairly clear content, and one has at least some idea of how to approach them. One can look forward to significant progress, I think.

M.R.:   Do you think that a new type of formalization would enable us to see language from a totally different viewpoint? For the moment we conceive of sentences as sequences of concatenated elements, that is to say, one placed after the other. Suppose that certain facts tend to prove that this perspective (which is expressed in the rewriting rules) is not the right one, and that we must consider sentences as "discontinuous" sequences: that certain elements can be inserted *between* other elements. Concretely that would be the same as saying that the rewriting rules take over a certain number of tasks presently assigned to transformations: permutations, inversions, adjunctions, and so on. Formally, these are models of insertion (intrication) . . .

N.C.: I personally began with something quite close to that, that is, with a much richer system of base rules and no transformations, in the work on Hebrew that we discussed. So naturally I don't regard this proposal as incoherent or out of the question. Such systems are certainly possible. One cannot be dogmatic in this matter. It is necessary to keep an open mind.

There are also other possibilities. It might be argued that a grammar is a bundle of perceptual strategies relating sound to meaning. That's a perspective very different from the one we've been discussing. It is conceivable that we will ultimately discover that this is the right approach—although I think that we have nothing to support such a belief today.

Once again, in the domain of embarrassing questions, I can see one that relates to your question about base grammar. There are languages where no argument has been found to justify one or another ordering of categories at the level of deep structure. These are languages of relatively free word order. The phenomenon is very interesting, although as yet inadequately described. There are languages where word order seems really to be much freer than in those languages usually called languages with a free word order—like Latin or Russian—which one can describe with rules like the "scrambling" rule* . . .

M.R.: Yes. In Russian or Latin, in spite of everything, word order is subjected to precise rules; and moreover, this involves nuances of semantic interpretation and of presupposition.

N.C.: This question has been studied by Ken Hale, who found such freedom of word order in Walbiri that he was obliged to attribute to such languages grammars of a sort that had occasionally been proposed, where the order of the base is free . . .

---

*The "scrambling rule" is a rule proposed by Ross to explain the inversions and permutations of Latin.

M.R.:   Like the applicational grammar of Šaumjan.

N.C.:   Yes, this requires other kinds of rules, perhaps non-linguistic ones, but involving such notions as "new information," etc. The grammar itself would leave word order fairly free. At least one can imagine this. Then one can ask: Are there actually two types of languages, quite different? Or is there a super-system, of which the two types are species? These are crucial questions, which are far from being clearly understood.

M.R.:   In effect, if two types of languages are possible, this casts doubt on the idea of a universal grammar.

In conclusion, you think that linguistics, in spite of all the problems that remain to be resolved, is the only positive element within the whole range of human sciences, except for a psychology of the future. However, there is one domain of which you have not spoken—generative poetics, which was created by Halle and Keyser at the end of the 1960s.[1] This competely new discipline can be considered a "human science": it meets all of your requirements. It has defined its object and its principles, it has provided itself with a theory of interaction between systems (the relation between literature and language), it has defined its concept of poetic competence. Born of generative grammar, it is not so much applied linguistics as structural poetics was. In my view this is also a field which has a rich future.

N.C.:   All this work is very interesting. However, I have contributed nothing to it, and do not feel qualified to discuss it. Here I have no competence at all; it is one of the innumerable subjects about which I have nothing to say . . .

Notes

Part I. LINGUISTICS AND POLITICS

Chapter 1. *Politics*

1. In *Liberation* (January 1973).
2. See *Ramparts* (April 1973); *Social Policy* (September 1973).
3. This appeared in the last number of that journal, which was not able to find financial support and no longer exists. *Ramparts,* August 1975.
4. See Dave Dellinger, *More Power Than We Know* (New York: Doubleday, 1975); and N. Chomsky, Introduction to N. Blackstock, ed., *Cointelpro* (New York: Vintage Books, 1976), for some examples.
5. *The New Industrial State* (New York: Signet Books, 1967), p. 335.
6. Manuel Uribe, *Le livre noir de l'intervention américaine au Chile* (Paris: Le Seuil, 1974).
7. Jean Pierre Faye, *Le Portugal d'Otelo: La révolution dans le labyrinthe* (Paris: J.-C. Lattès, 1976), contains an analysis of the reporting on the November 1975 coup in Portugal.
8. Morris Halle and S. Jay Keyser, *English Stress, Its Form, Its Growth and Its Role in Verse* (New York: Harper & Row, 1971), and "Chaucer and the Study of Prosody," *College English,* vol. 28 (1966), pp. 187–219.

Chapter 2. *Linguistics and the Human Sciences*

1. William Labov, *Language in the Inner City—Studies in Black English Vernacular* (Philadelphia: University of Pennsylvania Press, 1972); also *The Study of Non-Standard English* (Urbana, Ill.: University of Illinois Press, 1975).
2. See Basil Bernstein, *Langages et classes sociales* (Paris: Editions de Minuit, 1975).

Chapter 3. *A Philosophy of Language?*

1. E. J. Dijksterhuis, *The Mechanization of the World Picture* (London: Oxford University Press, 1961), p. 466.

2. The text appears in Fons Elders, ed., *Reflexive Waters* (London: Souvenir Press, 1974).

Chapter 4. *Empiricism and Rationalism*

1. See especially *Word and Object* (Cambridge, Mass.: MIT Press, 1960).
2. See Chomsky, *Reflections on Language,* for a detailed discussion.

Part II.   GENERATIVE GRAMMAR
Chapter. 5. *The Birth of Generative Grammar*

1. (Cambridge, Mass.: MIT Press, 1975) and (Englewood Cliffs, N.J.: Prentice-Hall, 1977), respectively.
2. Otto Jespersen, *A Modern English Grammar on Historical Principles* (Heidelberg: 1909–49).
3. The first collaborator of Chomsky, who played a primary role in developing the generative phonology of Russian and English, and later a generative theory of the structure of poetry.
4. A specialist in the psychology of language and its biological basis.
5. See his *Methods in Structural Linguistics* (Chicago: University of Chicago Press, 1951), available in manuscript in 1947. My own introduction to linguistics was through proof-reading this MS in 1947.
6. Troubetskoy was founder, with Roman Jakobson, of the Prague Circle. See his *Principles of Phonology,* translated by C. A. M. Baltaxe (Berkeley, Calif.: University of California Press, 1969).
7. See especially his "A Set of Postulates for Phonemic Analysis," *Language,* vol. 37 (1948).
8. See his *Anleitung zu phonologischen Beschreibungen* (Göttingen: Vandenhoeck-Ruprecht, 1935).
9. Z. S. Harris, "Transformational Theory," *Language,* vol. 41 (1965).
10. See N. Chomsky, "Formal Properties of Grammar," and G. A. Miller and N. Chomsky, "Finitary Models of Language Users," both in R. D. Luce, R. Bush, and E. Galanter, eds., *Handbook of Mathematical Psychology,* vol. II (New York: Wiley, 1963); N. Chomsky and M. P. Schützenberger, "The Algebraic Theory of Context-Free Languages," in P. Braffort and D. Hirschberg, eds., *Computer Programming and Formal Systems: Studies in Logic* (Amsterdam, North Holland: 1963); S. Ginsberg, *The Mathematical Theory of Context-Free Languages* (New York: McGraw-Hill, 1966); J. Hopcroft and J. D. Ullman, *Formal Languages and Their Relation to Automata* (Cambridge, Mass.: Addison-Wesley Press, 1969); J. Kimball, *The Formal Theory of Grammar* (Englewood Cliffs, N.J.: Prentice-Hall, 1973); and M. Gross and A. Lentin, *Introduction to Formal Grammars* (New York: Springer-Verlag, 1970).
11. (Holland: Mouton, 1964).

Chapter 6. *Semantics*

1. *Semantic Interpretation in Generative Grammar* (Cambridge, Mass.: MIT Press, 1972).

Chapter 8. *Deep Structure*

1. "French Relative Clauses," an unpublished Ph.D. thesis, MIT, Cambridge, Mass., 1974.

Chapter 9. *Universal Grammar and Unresolved Questions*

1. See Halle and Keyser, *English Stress: Its Form, Its Growth and Its Role in Verse* (New York: Harper & Row, 1971); and "Chaucer and the Study of Prosody," *College English* (December 1966).

Index

abduction, 71

academic world: and U.S. foreign policy, 41. *See also* universities

accessibility and accessible theories, 65–67, 76

ACLU, 25, 26

active-passive relationship, 106, 121, 123, 151n; in Harris's framework, 120–1. *See also* passive; transformations and transformational grammar

adolescence, 98

Akmajian, Adrian: *Introduction to the Principles of Transformational Syntax,* 104

All God's Dangers (Rosengarten), 55

Alperovitz, Gar, 16

American foreign policy, 6, 40–41; Cambodia, 24; Chile, 34, 35, 40; Cold War, 15–17; economic bases, 41; Laos, 10, 30; reconstruction of belief in, 35–36. *See also* Vietnam War

American Intellectual Elite, The (Kadushin), 11

American intellectuals, *see* intellectuals and intelligentsia

American mass media, 6, 19; "balance" policy, 8–9; as capitalistic institutions, 9; social and political analysis in, 6, 7–8; subservience of, 9–10; "vaccination" policy, 34–35. *See also* press

Amin, Idi, 34

anaphora and anaphoric relations, 142, 145, 147, 185; bound, 185

anarcho-syndicalists, 74

anthropology, 59–60

aphasia, 53

applicational grammar, 193

artificial intelligence, 128–9

artificial language, 70

artists, 76

Aspects of the Theory of Syntax (Chomsky), 136, 150, 151, 163, 169

Austin, John, 72, 132, 144

Australia, 7; aborigines, 59–60

autocracy, 91

automata theory, 125

autonomy of syntax, 138–9, 140, 148, 188–9; Jespersen on, 156

Baker, C. L.: *Introduction to Generative Transformational Syntax,* 104

Bar-Hillel, Yehoshua, 130

base component, 104–6, 119, 165, 169, 170; in Chomsky's second model, 136. *See also* rewriting rules behavior, 142; empirical approach, 68–69; technological approaches, 128; verbal, 129

behaviorism and behavioral science, 84, 128, 129; Chomsky's critique of, 46–47, 49, 113–14

beliefs: semantic role of, 142–3, 144, 147–8, 152–3, 189

Bernstein, Basil, 56

"Best Theory, The" (Postal), 150

Bever, Thomas, 53, 151, 154

biological constraints: on cognitive systems, 84, 94, 98–99; on knowledge, 63–68; on language, 98; theory construction role of, 64–69, 76–77. See also universal grammar

biology of language, 133

Black English, 53–56

Black Panthers, 21–24

Blackstone Rangers, 21–24

Bloch, Bernard, 118, 130

Bloomfield, Leonard: Menomini Morphophonemics, 112

body, 81, 83, 84; empirical view, 81–82

Bolshevism, 74, 90

Bracken, Harry, 92–93, 94

brain: empirical view, 81–82; genetic code and, 84. See also cognitive structures and systems

Brazil, 40

Bresnan, Joan, 172

California: FBI activities, 25–26

Cambodia, 24

Canada, 7

capitalism, 9, 12–13, 70; role of intelligentsia in, 90–91

Cartesian Linguistics (Chomsky), 77–78

Cartesianism, 176; dualism, 92–93, 96–97; innésism, 94; mechanics, 96; soul concept, 96–97. See also Descartes, René

case grammars, 154–6, 157

censorship, 20, 21, 24, 26, 30–31; national patterns, 31; Solzhenitsyn on, 32. See also ideological control

Central Intelligence Agency (CIA), 29

Chicago, 25, 26, 31, 158; FBI activity in, 21–24, 25

Chile: U.S. intervention in, 34, 35, 40

China, 15, 17

Chomsky, Noam: Aspects of the Theory of Syntax, 136, 150, 151, 163, 169; Cartesian Linguistics, 77–78; Counterrevolutionary Violence: Bloodbaths in Fact and Propaganda, 20, 37–38; Current Issues in Linguistic Theory, 134, 182; Foucault and, 74–80; Language and Mind, 49; lecture to Nieman Fellows, 30–31; letter to New York Times on Vietnam War, 37–38; as linguistics teacher, 134–5; link between linguistic and political activities, 3–8; Logical Structure of Linguistic Theory (LSLT), 106, 108–11, 113–14, 122–5, 126, 131–2, 138, 139, 140, 151n, 170, 175, 182, 183; "Morphophonemics of Modern Hebrew," 111–12, 130; objections to empiricism, 81–83; philosophical influences on, 70–74, 132; political writings, 30; "Questions on Form and Interpretation," 156–7; Reflections on Grammar, 61n; Reflections on Language, 61n, 63, 92, 160, 172; "Remind," 154; Syntactic Structures, 110, 113, 127, 131, 133, 136, 138, 139, 140, 144, 145, 151n, 175; work on history of ideas, 77. See also generative grammar

Church Committee, 21, 24, 26

Citizens' Commission to Investigate the FBI, 22

civil rights movement, 14, 27

Clark, Mark, 23

class struggle, 80

Clemens, Diane, 15

cognitive grammar, 150, 153

cognitive psychology, 109, 111, 113, 114, 116; emerging discipline of, 134; linguistics and, 43–53; and psychology of language, 44–46. *See also* psychology of language

cognitive structures and systems, 45, 49, 64, 126; analogies between, 83–84; biological constraints on, 84, 94, 98–99; compared to physiological structures, 84, 86, 87; interactions between, 48, 49, 143, 147, 165; language as, 165; as mental organs, 82–83, 180–1; organizational complexity of, 81; performance vs. competence models, 48–51; role in meaning and reference, 142, 143, 145; study of, 49, 82–84, 116–17; vision, 45, 46, 49, 51–52. *See also* brain; cognitive psychology; knowledge; mind

Cointelpro, 22–28

Colby, William, 30

cold war, 15–17

colonial system, 92, 93

communication: as goal of language, 85–88; mathematical theory of, 125, 127, 128

Communist Control Act, 28

Communists and Communist party, 28, 29, 32; FBI disruption attempts, 26–27. *See also* Marxism

competence, 57; grammatical, 150; linguistic, 48–49, 56; poetic, 194

competence models: vs. performance models, 48–50; for vision, 51

computers, 128, 129

conceptual change, 171

conditioning, 85

consciousness, 96

co-reference, 146–7, 163, 175

Council on Foreign Relations, 41

Counterrevolutionary Violence: Bloodbaths in Fact and Propaganda (Chomsky and Herman), 20, 37–38

Course of Modern Linguistics (Hockett), 169

covert categories, 169

creativity, 96, 156, 178–9; Chomsky vs. Foucault on, 75–76; Humboldt's concepts, 78

Crisis of Democracy, The (Crozier et al.), 17

Crozier, Michel, 17

Current Issues in Linguistic Theory (Chomsky), 134, 182

cybernetics, 128

Czechoslovakia, 34

Davidson, Donald, 72

Davis, Angela, 34

death: genetic determination of, 98–99

deduction, 71

deep structure, 136, 137, 148, 150, 151, 152, 163, 165, 167, 168, 169–79, 193; in Extended Standard Theory, 171–2; and grammatical relations, 173–4; history of, 169–73; innate, 171; misconceptions of, 171–2; properties of, 170; and semantics, 172; in Standard Theory, 169–70, 173; term, 169; and universal grammar, 183–4

democracy: propaganda in, 38–39

Democratic party, 21

derivational constraints, 150–1

Descartes, René, 66, 76, 78, 156; theory of the soul, 96–97. *See also* Cartesianism

descriptive linguistics, 108, 114. *See also* structuralism

descriptive semantics, 155

descriptivism, 148–9

dialects, 53–56; unresolved questions, 190–2

Dijksterhuis, E. J., 78, 79

discourse, 146, 147

discourse analysis, 120–1

discovery procedures, 114–16, 117, 118–19, 130–1; automation of, 129

Dominican Republic, 35
Donner, Frank, 26
Dougherty, Ray, 151, 154, 155
Dumke, Glenn, 26
Dummett, Michael, 72

economics: of American foreign policy, 41; colonial system, 92, 93; student challenges to, 18
education, 54–55
empiricism, 81–99, 107, 129, 154; approach to acquisition of knowledge, 71; functionalism, 85–88; in generative grammar, 117; ideological and social factors, 88–93; inadequacies of, 68–69, 71; methodological dualism of, 82, 83, 92; Piaget's, 84–85; in psychology, 50; and structural linguistics, 116–17, 118
empiricist learning theory, 126, 127–8
engineers, 125
English language, 59, 146, 174; accentuation of sentences in, 172; active-passive relationships, 106, 121, 123, 150–1; auxiliary system, 110, 111; generative phonology of, 133, 135; nominalizations, 135; non-standard, 53–55; passive, 158–62; reflexivation, 185–7; traditional grammars, 61
epistemology, 71, 73, 114
Europe, 191
European Marxism, 74–80
European philosophers, 73
evaluation procedures, 112, 113, 114, 117, 118
evolution, 86, 87
experimental method, 46–47
experimental psychology, 46–47
Extended Standard Theory, 151–2, 154, 163–8, 182; deep structure, 171–2; logical form, 165–6; rewriting rules, 163; surface structure position, 163–4; trace theory,

164–5. *See also* generative grammar

Fascist countries, 11
Faye, Jean Pierre, 5, 8, 34
Federal Bureau of Investigation (FBI), 21–27, 29, 31; basic function, 22; Cointelpro operations, 22–28; role in Black Panther assassinations, 21–24
Feis, Herbert, 16
Fiengo, Robert, 160, 164
Fillmore, Charles, 148–9; case grammars, 154–6
Fleming, D. F., 15, 19
focus, 164
Fodor, Jerry, 44–45, 135, 136
Fodor-Katz hypothesis, 140–3
Ford, Gerald, 34
foreign accents, 98
formalization, 192
Foucault, Michel, 74–80; on creativity, 75–76; on human nature, 75, 77; politics of, 80; as structuralist, 76–77
France, 47, 71, 135, 148, 154. *See also* French language
free expression, 156
Frege, Gottlob, 142
French language, 98, 103, 157, 162; co-reference, 146; syntax, 183; transformation, 106
French philosophy, 73, 74
French Romantics, 70
French Syntax (Kayne), 106n
functionalism, 85–88

Galbraith, John Kenneth, 15; *The New Industrial State,* 15, 16, 17
Galileo (Galilei), 107, 108
generative grammar, 3, 46, 69, 155, 183; base component (rewriting rules), 104–5, 119, 170; classical precedents, 112; concerns and goals of, 109–11, 140; creativity inherent in, 178–9; deep structure, 169–79; degrees of grammatical-

ness, 175; empirical hypotheses, 117; evaluation procedures, 112, 113, 114, 117, 118; Extended Standard Theory, 151–2, 154, 163–8, 171–2; of factual knowledge, 143; first students and researchers, 134–5; history of, 106, 134–5, 137; kernel sentences, 170; linguists' response to, 94, 130–4; and meaning, 137, 140–1, 142; of Modern Hebrew, 111–12, 130, 133, 193; opposition to structuralism, 106–19; vs. relational grammar, 156; review of properties of, 103–6; semantics component, 137–62; sociolinguists' view, 191–2; specified subject condition, 61; Standard Theory, 135, 137, 141, 148, 150–2, 154, 163, 169–70, 173; surface structure, 170, 175–7; transformation theory, 119–24, 136, 181–2; unresolved questions, 184–94; vision analogy, 51–52. *See also* Chomsky, Noam; grammar

generative phonology, 111, 133, 135, 178

generative poetics, 194

generative semantics, 148–54, 171; global rules, 152; idealization in, 152, 153; and neo-Bloomfieldian descriptivism, 154; surface structure position, 164

"Generative Semantics" (Lakoff), 150

German Romantics, 70

Germany, 148

Gestalt psychology, 47

global rules, 152

Goodman, Nelson, 72, 130, 132, 137, 140–1

grammar, 44, 48, 51, 189; applicational, 193; as autonomous mental organ, 83, 85, 97–98; case, 154–6, 157; cognitive, 150, 153; compared to universal grammar, 183–4; components of, 181; co-reference principles, 146–7, 163, 175; defining concepts, 138; derivational constraints, 150; French, 103; of generative semanticists, 152; as illegitimate idealization, 189; implicit knowledge of, 103–4, 109, 111; "interesting" phenomena, 60–61; vs. language, 97–98; morphophonological component, 105; of a natural language, 105, 126; non-discrete, 149, 153; non-linguistic factors, 152–3; phrase structure, 112, 127; relational, 149, 156, 157–62; rewriting rules, 104–6; role of semantics in, 137–40; of sentences, 120, 147; sociolinguistics and, 190–1; traditional, 103, 108, 109, 140, 154, 157, 187; transformational, 44–45, 105–6, 110, 111, 127, 181; universal, *see* universal grammar; unresolved questions, 193–4. *See also* generative grammar; grammatical relations; grammatical rules

grammatical competence, 150

grammatical relations, 157; between structural positions, 173–4

grammatical rules, 158–9, 181, 189; derivational constraints, 150–1; NP-movement, 159–60, structure-preserving, 160

grammaticality, 138

grammaticalness: degrees of, 175

gravity, 96

Greek, 186

Gregory, Richard: vision experiments, 51

Grevisse, M., 103

Grice, Paul, 72

Gruber, J., 154

Hale, Kenneth, 59–60, 193

Halle, Morris, 42, 48, 56, 113, 131, 132, 133, 135, 194

Hampton, Fred, 23, 24, 31

Harris, Zellig, 115, 116, 117, 118, 132; *Methods,* 118, 120, 122;

transformational theory, 112, 119–24

Harvard University, 30, 127, 128, 129, 131, 132, 133

Hebrew: generative grammar, 111–12, 130, 133, 193

Helke, Michael, 185

Heny, Frank: *Introduction to the Principles of Transformational Syntax*, 104

Herman, Edward S., 37–38

hermeneutics, 174

Hill, Archibald, 133

Hintikka, Jaakko, 73

history of ideas: Chomsky's approach, 77–79

history of science, 65, 73; hindsight in, 78–79

Hockett, Charles, 115, 118, 125; *Course in Modern Linguistics*, 169

Hoenigswald, Henry, 130

Horowitz, David, 15

Human Knowledge (Russell), 71–72

human nature, 68, 70, 91; behaviorist concepts, 128; Cartesian view, 92–93; Chomsky vs. Foucault on, 75, 77; concepts and social science theory, 70; denial of, 90–91; empirical view, 90–92, 93; uniqueness of, 94–95. *See also* biological constraints; universal grammar

human reason, 66

human sciences, 57, 59, 128, 194. *See also* social sciences

humanities, 175, 177, 178

Humboldt, Wilhelm von, 78, 109, 135, 156

Hume, David, 82

Humphrey, Hubert, 28

Huntington, Samuel, 17

idealization, 54, 55–56, 57–58, 61, 189; and generative semantics, 152, 153; legitimate, 142–3; in natural sciences, 73

ideological censorship, 21, 24, 26, 30–31

ideological control, 9, 11, 17, 21, 28, 31, 38

ideology, 154; empiricism and, 88–93

imperialism, 191

Indonesia, 40

induction, 71, 72, 85; Hume's view, 82

infants: perceptual systems of, 52–53

inflectional morphology, 174

information theory, 125

initial phrase marker, 172

innéisme, 85

intellectual tasks, 80

intellectuals and intelligentsia, 5, 90; analytical role of, 4–5; capitalist, 90–91; and empiricism, 89–90, 91, 93; and generative grammar, 154; and ideological control, 9, 11, 28, 31; mainstream, 32; post-Vietnam, 35; socialist, 90; Spanish, 11; technocratic, 90

intelligence, 95, 103, 128–9; artificial, 128–9

International Congress of Linguists, 133–4

International Journal of American Linguistics, 115

interpretive components, 136

interpretive rules, 168

Introduction to Generative Transformational Syntax (Baker), 104

Introduction to the Principles of Transformational Syntax (Akmajian and Heny), 104

Jackendoff, Ray, 145, 151, 152, 156, 163, 164, 185

Jackson, Robert, 29

Jakobson, Roman, 77, 118, 125

Japan and the Japanese, 7, 18, 186

Jespersen, Otto, 156–7; free expressions, 109; *Philosophy of Grammar*, 156; and relational grammar, 157–62

Johnson, Lyndon B., 34

Joos, Martin, 76

Journal of Symbolic Logic, 131

justice, 80

Kadushin, C.: *The American Intellectual Elite,* 11
Kasher, Asa, 73
Katz, Jerrold, 72, 135, 136, 140–3, 144, 145, 148, 154
Kayne, Richard, 183; *French Syntax,* 106n
Kendall, Walter, 90
Kennedy, John F., 34
Kennedy, Robert, 27
Keyser, S. Jay, 42, 194
kinship systems, 60
Kissinger, Henry, 10
Klima, Edward, 134, 135
knowledge, 83, 84; biological constraints on, 63–68; empirical view, 116; Foucault's theory, 75–76; linguistic, 103–4, 109, 111, 113, 114, 116, 124, 140, 189; mathematical, 67–68; musical, 68; Piaget's view, 84–85; scientific, 75. *See also* cognitive structures and systems; philosophy of knowledge
Köhler, Wolfgang, 47
Kolko, Gabriel, 15, 19
Korean language, 186
Kripke, Saul, 72
Ku Klux Klan, 27
Kuhn, Thomas, 73

Labov, William, 53–56
Lakatós, Imre, 73
Lakoff, George, 148, 150, 154, 189; "Generative Semantics," 150
Langages, 154
language, 48, 51; artificial, 70; as aspect of human nature, 77, 95–96; behavioral analogue, 69; biology of, 94, 98, 133; as cognitive system, 83, 165; creative aspect of, 156; definition of, 190; discovery procedures, 114–16; explanatory theory, 106–7, 109–10, 111–12, 114, 122, 124, 131; facts of, 142, 166; functionalist view, 85–88; of the ghettos, *see* Black English; individual spoken, 54; infinity of forms, 64; "interesting" phenomena in, 59,

60–62; Markov source models, 125–26, 127, 129; as model of knowledge, 63–65; natural, 73, 105, 126, 166, 167; neurology of, 48, 53; perceptual influences on, 44–45, 84; and power, 191; psychological assumptions about, 50; Saussurean theory, 50, 51, 97–98; social interaction analogue, 69–70; of Stone Age man, 55; structuralist view, 76–77; structure of, 167; uses of, 87–88; word order, 193. *See also* grammar; language acquisition; language use; linguistic theory; linguistics; syntactic structure

Language, 46, 113, 122, 133
language acquisition, 43, 44, 50, 113, 114, 117, 124, 180; and autonomy of syntax, 138–9; boundary conditions, 111–12, 116, 117; critical age for, 98; discovery procedures, 114–16; empirical view, 85; functionalist view, 86–87; and generative semantics, 148; mechanism of, 98. *See also* language; linguistics
Language and Mind (Chomsky), 49
language change, 87
language games, 60
language use, 144, 153; Oxford theories, 141
Laos, 10, 30
Laplace, Pierre Simon de, 96
lateralization, 53
Latin, 193
learning theory, 126; empiricist, 126, 127–8
Lees, Robert, 113, 133, 134, 135
leftists, 19, 20, 27, 90. *See also* Communists and Communist party; Marxism
Leibniz, Gottfried Wilhelm von, 143
Lenin, Nikolai, 90
Leninist doctrine, 74
Lenneberg, Eric, 113, 133
Lévi-Strauss, Claude, 60
lexical insertion, 169, 170, 174
lexical items, 169, 170, 173–4

lexical passive, 161

lexical rules, 181

lexicon, 136, 137

liberals and liberalism: classical, 70; concept of human nature, 70; Democratic, 28; ideology, 35; intellectuals, 15–17; and McCarthyism, 28–29; press, 24, 31–32, 33, 35–40; repressive actions of, 28–29; retrospective analyses of Vietnam War, 35–40; Solzhenitsyn and, 31–32, 33. *See also* American mass media; press

linguistic competence, 48–49; of lower-class children, 56

linguistic judgments, 153

linguistic levels, 139

Linguistic Society of America, 157

linguistic structure, 183; and perception, 44–45, 47–48

linguistic theory, 106–10, 111–12, 114, 122, 124, 130, 131, 152, 154–5; as goal of generative grammar, 109–10; innate, 140; pre-generative grammar, 167; semantic considerations, 139; and theory of ideology, 41–42; and universal grammar, 183–4. *See also* universal grammar

linguistic universals, 76–77

linguistics, 64, 178–9, 188; activities and concerns, 61, 118–19; American neo-Bloomfieldian, 76; and anthropology, 59–60; Chomsky's view, 194; and cognitive psychology, 43–53, 122, 134; competence concept, 57; competence models, 48–50; descriptive, 108, 114; and early generative grammar, 130–4; formalization, 125; functionalism, 85–88; goals of, 148, 153; idealization in, 54, 55–56, 57–58, 61; and ideology, 190–4; limitations of, 48; and mathematics, 6, 124–9; politics and, 3–8; as science, 106–9; and

social dominance, 57; and sociology, 53–59; structuralism, *see* structuralism; study of dialects, 53–56; study of meaning and reference, 139. *See also* language; linguistic structure; linguistic theory; psycholinguistics; psychology of language; sociolinguistics

literary criticism, 56–57

literature, 194

Locke, John, 92

logic, 156, 166–7; of conversation, 72; and language theory, 167; and universal grammar, 183

logical form, 145, 165–8, 189; derivational process, 166

Logical Structure of Linguistic Theory, The (Chomsky), 106, 108–11, 113–14, 126, 138, 139, 140, 151n, 170, 175, 182, 183; reception of, 131–2; transformation theory, 122–5

Lukoff, Fred, 135

Luxemburg, Rosa, 74

machine translation, 135

markedness, 118

Markov source models, 125–6, 127, 129

Marshall, George, 29

Marx, Karl, 70, 91

Marxism, 18, 74; Bolshevism, 74, 90; Chomsky on, 74; political economy, 58

Massachusetts Institute of Technology (MIT), 25, 131, 132, 185, 186; linguistics department, 134; research climate, 132–3; Research Laboratory of Electronics, 132, 134, 135

mass media, *see* American mass media; press

materialism, 94

mathematical linguistics, 6, 127

mathematical theory of communication, 125, 127, 128

mathematics, 60, 67–68; compared to political science, 7; and linguistics, 124–9; non-demonstrative inference, 71–72

Matthews, G. H., 134, 135

Mattick, Paul, 74

maturation, 82, 94, 98

McCarran Act, 28

McCarthy, Joseph, 28–29

McCawley, James, 148

meaning, 72, 106, 140–2, 165; Chomsky's theory, 140–1; deep structure and, 163; dual theory of, 140–1; related to form, 150; sentences devoid of, 144; surface structure and, 151–2; and syntax, 137, 138–9; and universal grammar, 140. *See also* semantics and semantic theory

meaningfulness, 138

mechanics: Cartesian vs. Newtonian, 96–97; classical, 78

Mehler, Jacques, 47

memory, 48, 49, 86, 97, 98

Menomini Morphophonemics (Bloomfield), 112

mental faculties, *see* cognitive structures and systems; mental organs; mind

mental organs, 83, 180–1, 189; grammar as, 83, 85, 97–98. *See also* cognitive structures and systems

Methods (Harris), 118, 120, 122

metrics, 42, 48

Middle East, 6–7

Miller, George, 86, 129, 133

mind: as biological system, 66; Chomsky's view, 83; empirical view, 82; innate structures, 94. *See also* brain; cognitive structures and systems

mind-body dualism, 81–83

minorities, 21

Minute Men, 24–25

model of competence, 189–90

model-theoretic semantics, 72

Montague, Richard: quantification theory, 167, 168

Moravcsik, Julius, 72, 141

Morgenthau, Hans, 11

"Morphophonemics of Modern Hebrew" (Chomsky), 111–13, 130, 133

morphophonology, 105, 136

Moynihan, Daniel P., 33–34

music, 68

Nation, 26

natural history, 58–59, 78–79, 178

natural language, 73; grammar of, 105, 126; quantifiers in, 166; syntax of, 167

natural sciences, 66, 81; concerns of, 58–59; idealization in, 57–58, 73; vs. natural history, 58–59; progress in, 73, 171, 175–6, 187–8; theories, 122. *See also* physics

Nazism, 5

negation and negative structures, 151, 161, 163

neurological structures and functions, 48; lateralization, 53. *See also* brain

New Industrial State, The (Galbraith), 15, 16, 17

New Left, 19, 27

New Republic, 24

"New Taxonomy, The" (Fillmore), 148

New York Times, 19; retrospective analysis of Vietnam War, 36–38

Newton, Isaac, 78

Nixon, Richard M.: 20–21, 24, 27–28, 29, 34; enemies list, 21, 24. *See also* Watergate affair

non-demonstrative inference, 71–72

non-discrete grammar, 149, 153

number theory, 67

O'Neal, William, 23

Otero, Carlos, 174

Ottoman Empire, 191
Panini: grammar of Sanskrit, 112
Pannekoek, Anton, 74
passive: lexical, 161
passive-active dichotomy, 151n.
    See also active-passive relationship
passive transformation, 158–62, 182n
Paul, Hermann, 109
peace movement, 27, 37, 38
Peirce, Charles Sanders, 71
Pentagon Papers, 41
perception and perceptual systems, 52–53, 189; of infants, 52–53; and sentence structure, 44–45, 84; visual, 45, 46, 49, 51–53. *See also* cognitive structures and systems
performance models, 48, 49, 50, 189–90. *See also* behaviorism and behavioral science
Peters, Stanley, 127
philosophy and philosophers, 70–79, 85, 132, 134, 138, 167; Cartesian dualism, 92–93, 96–97; empiricism, *see* empiricism; Marxist-Leninist, 74–80. *See also* philosophy of knowledge; philosophy of language; philosophy of science
Philosophy of Grammar (Jespersen), 156
philosophy of knowledge, 63; Hume, 82; Piaget's, 84–85; Russell's theories, 71–72; theory construction, 64–67. *See also* knowledge; philosophy and philosophers
philosophy of language, 63–65, 72–73; contemporary, 72–73; Jespersen, 156; and universal language, 183. *See also* language; linguistics; philosophy and philosophers
philosophy of science, 63–64, 73; biological constraint concepts, 65–68; creativity concepts, 75–76; theory construction, 65–67, 71. *See also* natural sciences; physics

phoneme, 138, 177
phonetics and phonetic representation, 165, 189; and semantics, 141
phonology, 112, 118, 130, 139, 152, 155, 164, 166, 167, 172, 173, 175, 184, 189; generative, 111, 133, 135, 178; structuralist vs. generative, 178; trace, 175
phrase markers, 158, 170, 172
phrase structure grammar, 112, 127
physics, 66, 129, 153, 172, 188; experimental techniques, 47; Galilean, 107, 108; "interesting" phenomena for, 58–59; mechanics, 78, 96–97; as model for linguistics, 106, 107–8. *See also* natural sciences
physiology, 83, 84
Piaget, Jean, 46; empiricism, of, 84–85
P-marker, *see* phrase marker
poetic competence, 194
poetry, 175
Polish language, 186
politics, 3–42; Chomsky vs. Foucault on, 79–80; linguistics and, 3–8; student movement, 12–20. *See also* American foreign policy; liberals and liberalism; United States; Vietnam War; Watergate affair
Popper, Karl, 71
Port-Royal *Grammaire Générale,* 76, 168
Portuguese intellectuals, 11
Postal, Paul, 135, 136, 148, 149, 156, 158; "The Best Theory," 150
pragmatics, 73, 149
Pravda, 9
press: American liberal, 24, 31–32, 33, 35–40; ideological censorship of, 21, 24, 26, 30–31; in Vietnam War, 9–11, 35–40; in Watergate affair, 30, 31. *See also* American mass media
presupposition, 164
Princeton: Institute for Advanced Study, 133

process models, 48
projection rules, 137, 144
propaganda systems, 38–39
propositions, 167, 168
psycholinguistics, 44, 47–48, 133; concerns of, 47–48; Fodor's "click" experiments, 44–45; and social discrimination, 56. *See also* psychology of language
psychological reality, 118, 119; of discovery procedures, 115, 116
psychology, 60, 114, 125, 134, 194; behavioral, *see* behaviorism and behavioral sciences; Chomsky's paradigm for, 49; cognitive, 44–46, 109, 111, 113, 114, 116, 134; empiricism in, 50; experimental, 46–47; Gestalt, 47; and linguistics, 43–53; need for competence concept, 49. *See also* psycholinguistics; psychology of language
psychology of language, 44–50, 84; vs. behaviorism, 46–47; field of study of, 44; influence on other fields, 44–46; performance vs. competence models in, 48–50. *See also* cognitive psychology; psycholinguistics
Putnam, Hilary, 72

qualifiers, 142
quantifiers and quantification, 151, 163, 165, 166; Montague's theory of, 167, 168
"Questions of Form and Interpretation" (Chomsky), 156–7
Quine, W. V., 72, 85, 129, 130, 132, 137–8, 141, 143

racism, 92–93
raising, 44–45, 173–4
Ramparts, 10
rationalism, 77, 84. *See also* empiricism
reason, 66
reference, 140–2. *See also* co-reference; meaning

Reflections on Grammar (Chomsky), 61n
Reflections on Language (Chomsky), 61n, 63, 92, 160, 172
reflexivation, 185–7
relational grammar, 149, 156, 157–62
relative clauses, 173
"Remind" (Chomsky), 154
research, 57, 58
rewriting rules, 104–5, 110, 119, 136, 160, 181; derivational history of, 170; in Extended Standard Theory, 163
Ritchie, Robert, 127
Rocker, Rudolf, 74
Romantics, 70
Rosenbaum, Peter, 151
Rosengarten, Theodore: *All God's Dangers,* 55
Ross, John, 148, 149, 183, 189
Russell, Bertrand: *Human Knowledge,* 71–72
Russia: Cold War and, 15, 16, 17; Revolution, 74; Solzhenitsyn's view, 32. *See also* Soviet Union
Russian language, 193; generative phonology of, 135

Sakharov, Andrei, 32
Samuelson, Paul, 18
San Diego: Minute Men, 24–25, 31
San Diego State College, 25
Sapir, Edward, 118
Šaumjan, Sebastian, 167, 194
Saussurean system, 50, 51, 156; *langue* concept, 97–98
Schlesinger, Arthur, 17
Schützenberger, M. P., 127, 135
science, *see* empiricism; natural sciences; philosophy of science; physics
scientific creativity, 74–75
Seattle, 26
Secret Army Organization, 25, 31
Selkirk, Lisa, 164

semantic interpretation, 169, 170–1, 173; role of surface structure, 163. *See also* semantics and semantic theory

semantic representation, 141, 171; and deep structure, 148, 150–2; vs. logical form, 145; and surface structure, 150–2, 171, 173; and syntactic structures, 141; T-marker, 170; and truth conditions, 144–8. *See also* semantics and semantic theory

semantics and semantic theory, 106, 136–62, 164, 175, 184; co-reference principles, 146; and deep structure, 172; definitions of, 140; extensional vs. intensional, 144–5; Fodor-Katz hypothesis, 140–3; generative, 148–54, 164, 171; grammar role of, 137–40; integration of theory of, 154–6; interpretive, 145; linguistic theory role of, 139; model-theoretic, 72; of natural languages, 73; pre-Standard Theory, 137–8; projection rules, 144; and systems of belief, 142–3, 144, 147–8; universal, 140–3, 144. *See also* meaning; semantic representation

semiology, 71

sentences and sentence grammar, 120, 147; devoid of meaning, 144; negation and quantification, 151; perceptual influences on, 44–45, 84; relative clauses, 173–4; transformational history of, 170; truth and, 144–8

Shaw, Nate, 55

simplicity and simplicity measure, 112, 113, 130

Skinner, B. F., 46–47, 129

slavery, 91

Smith, Adam, 70

Smith, Gaddis, 19

SNCC (Student Non-violent Coordinating Committee), 14

social and political analysis, 4–5; credentials for, 6–7

social change, 70, 74, 80

social control, 90. *See also* ideological control

social interaction: universal grammar of, 69–70

social sciences, 6, 12; accessibility of, 4–5; conceptual change in, 175–6, 177–8; human nature concepts, 70–76. *See also* anthropology; human sciences; psychology; sociology

Socialist Workers party, 27

socialists and socialism: in American mass media, 9; intelligentsia and, 90. *See also* Marxism

sociolinguistics, 53–56, 57; questions about, 190–4; view of generative grammar, 191–2. *See also* linguistics; sociology

sociology, 192; Chomsky's view, 56–59; compared to natural sciences, 58–59; linguistics and, 53–59; methods, 58; resistance to idealization, 57–58

Solzhenitsyn, Alexander, 31–34

soul, 96–97

Soviet Union, 9, 32; American Communists and, 32, 34. *See also* Russia

Spain, 11, 32

spatial intuition, 67

speech acts, 72

Standard Theory, 135, 137, 141, 148, 150–2, 163; compared to Fillmore's case grammar, 154; criticized, 173; deep structure in, 169–70, 173; symmetry of, 173. *See also* Extended Standard Theory; generative grammar

stimulus-response learning theory, 126

Stone Age, 55, 95

structuralism, 76–77, 97, 130, 138, 148, 154, 156, 167; Chomsky's alleged return to, 175–7; contributions of, 114–15; discovery procedures of, 114–16; distinguished from Chomsky's approach, 103, 106–19; empiricism and, 116–17, 118; surface structure and, 175–7; transformation theory, 119–24

structuralist phonology, 178

structure of discourse, 120

student movement, 12–20; and Cold War theory, 16, 17–18; government provocateurs, 13, 18; isolation of, 28; major effect of, 13–14, 17; in the seventies, 19–20

Suppes, Patrick, 126

surface structure, 120, 123, 136, 169, 170, 172, 173; Chomsky's concepts criticized, 175–7; lexical insertion and, 174; logical form, 166–8; meaning role, 151–2; position, 163–4; properties of, 175; semantic role, 163; and structuralism, 175–7; trace theory, 171, 173

syntactic structure, 158; base-generated, 112; meaning and, 137, 138; relation to logical form, 166–8; and semantic representations, 141; study of, 155; traditional vs. structural approach, 108–9; transformational rules, 105–6. *See also* deep structure; surface structure; syntax; transformations and transformational grammar

Syntactic Structures (Chomsky), 110, 113, 127, 131, 133, 136, 138, 139, 140, 144, 145, 151n, 175

syntax, 149, 152, 164, 166, 184, 189; autonomy of, 138–39, 140, 148, 156, 188–9; of natural language, 167; theory of, 167. *See also* syntactic structure

temporal processes, 48

Teuber, Hans-Lukas, 134

Texas Conference, 114, 132, 133

thematic relations, 157–8, 163, 164–5

theory and theory construction, 85; abduction principle, 71; accessible, 65, 66, 67; of behavior, 68–69; biological constraints on, 64–69, 76–77; inaccessible, 67; of social change, 70; true, 65–66, 67. *See also* linguistic theory

T-marker, 170

traces and trace theory, 164–5, 167, 171, 173, 177; structuring effect of silence, 175

traditional grammars, 103, 108, 109, 140, 154, 157, 187. *See also* grammar

transformations and transformational grammar, 110, 111, 156, 169, 181; active-passive relationship as, 106, 158–62; current hypotheses, 181–2; empirical evidence, 124; generalized, 170; Harris's work, 112, 119–24; and idiosyncratic properties of words, 174; incorrigible, 124; mathematical investigation of, 127; raising, 44–45; 173–4; rules, 105–6, 174, 181–2; singulary, 170; in structural vs. generative grammar, 119–24; trace theory, 164, 165

trees, 119

Trilateral Commission, 17

Troubetskoy, Nikolai, 116, 117, 118

Truman, Harry S, 28

truth, 144–8; in theory, 65–66, 67

Uganda, 34

United States: civil rights movement, 14, 27; Cold War and, 15–17; ideological conformity in, 12; intelligentsia, 90; military interventions of, 35–40; political freedom in, 30–31; social and political analysis in, 6–9; Solzhenitsyn on, 32. *See also* American mass media

universal grammar, 44, 49, 50, 61, 106, 140, 171, 172, 180–4, 194; and deep structure, 183–4; goals, 181; knowledge of linguistics for, 183;

as linguistic theory, 183–4; of mathematics, 67–68; mental organ concept, 180–1; misunderstandings about, 183–4; of music, 68; of possible social interaction, 69; relationship to grammar, 183–4; of social interaction, 69–70; for theory construction, 65

universal semantics, 140–3, 144, 148

universities, 8, 12–20; laboratories, 15; political censorship in, 25–6; politicization of, 14–17; purges, 28; social science programs, 15; student movement, 12–20. *See also* intellectuals and intelligentsia

University of Pennsylvania, 130

Uribe, Manuel, 34

vaccination, 34

verbal behavior, 129

Vergnaud, Jean-Roger, 173

Viertel, John, 135

Vietnam War, 6, 7, 34; American policy in, 35–40; peace treaty negotiations, 10; Phoenix Program, 29; press and, 9–11, 36–38; resisters and deserters, 32–33; retrospective analysis of, 35–41; Solzhenitsyn's view of, 32

violence, 80

visual perception, 45, 49, 83; face-perception theory, 51–52; of infants, 52–53; and spoken language, 46

wage labor, 91

Walbiri language, 193

Wallace, Henry, 28

Warburg, James, 15

Warner Bros., 38

Washington Post, 21; on Vietnam War, 39–40

Wasow, Thomas, 164

Watanuki, Joji, 17

Watergate affair, 20–1, 24, 27–28, 30, 31, 34; in context of other political crimes, 20–27

Western Europe, 7, 12, 18

Wha-Chun Kim, 186

What Is to Be Done? (Lenin), 90

White, Morton, 132

Whorf, Benjamin Lee: covert categories, 169

William James lectures, 129

Williams, William Appleman, 15, 19

Wittgenstein, Ludwig, 138, 143, 171; deep grammar-surface grammar, 169

Word, 132

word order, 193

women, 91

Yale University, 130

Yngve, Victor, 135

About the Author

Professor Noam Chomsky, an eminent and revolutionary scholar in the field of linguistics, has in recent years become a figure of national attention through his brilliant criticism of American political life. He received his B.A., M.A., and Ph.D. from the University of Pennsylvania and was a Junior Fellow of the Society of Fellows at Harvard from 1951 to 1955. In 1955 he was appointed to the faculty of the Massachusetts Institute of Technology, where he is now Ferrari P. Ward Professor of Linguistics. In addition he has served as John Locke Lecturer at Oxford; as a visiting professor at the University of California, Los Angeles, and at Berkeley; and as a Research Fellow at the Institute for Advanced Study at Princeton and the Center for Cognitive Studies at Harvard.

Among the many works Professor Chomsky has written in his field are *The Logical Structure of Linguistic Theory, Syntactic Structures, Aspects of the Theory of Syntax, Cartesian Linguistics, Language and Mind,* and with Morris Halle, *Sound Pattern of English.* Recently his articles on political and historical themes have attracted widespread attention. Professor Chomsky is a member of the National Academy of Sciences, the American Academy of Arts and Sciences, the Deutsche Akademie der Naturforscher Leopoldina, the Utrecht Society of Arts and Sciences, and a Corresponding Fellow of the British Academy, as well as a member of numerous professional societies and of the Council of the International Confederation for Disarmament and Peace. His most recent books are *American Power and the New Mandarins, At War with Asia, Problems of Knowledge and Freedom: The Russell Lectures, Studies on Semantics in Generative Grammar, For Reasons of State, Peace in the Middle East?,* and *Reflections on Language.*